Women

Women and Forgiveness

BRIAN FROST

With an Introduction by
Dr Una Kroll

and a Preface by
Michael Mayne

Collins

FOUNT PAPERBACKS

First published in Great Britain
by Fount Paperbacks, London in 1990

Printed and bound in Great Britain by William Collins Sons &
Co. Ltd, Glasgow

Contents

Preface

On Monday 29th January 1649, the day before his execution, King Charles I was early at his devotions and he was visited by two of his children, the thirteen-year-old Princess Elizabeth and the eight-year-old Duke of Gloucester. That night Princess Elizabeth recorded what passed between them. "He told me", she wrote, "he had forgiven all his enemies, and hoped God would forgive them also, and commanded us, and all the rest of my brothers and sisters, to forgive them." Not for nothing had the King spent long hours in prison meditating on the manner in which Christ faced his Passion and his death.

Brian Frost has chosen to tell the story of Sybil Phoenix and Una O'Higgins O'Malley because these two women have also learned from the manner of Christ's dying the power of forgiveness in situations of great darkness, the one certain way in which the evil of racism or the evil of internecine violence may begin to be redeemed. His theme and theirs is summed up very simply in Kevin O'Higgins' dying words, as the blood drained from his terrible wounds, words which echo those of Christ: "I forgive my murderers."

The Introduction by Una Kroll is a thoughtful reflection on what constitutes the work of reconciliation. It is the ability to forgive and to receive forgiveness, and Dr Kroll raises the question of whether women may not have a distinctive role in the process of reconciliation. She analyses her own changed attitude on the occasions when she has experienced an honest, non-patronizing forgiveness in those she has hurt: "they let me know that they were hurt but refused to treat me as I had treated them". And certainly the force of that kind of response is borne out time and again in the lives of the Guyanan Sybil Phoenix in South London and the Irish Una O'Higgins O'Malley both in the Republic of Ireland and in Northern Ireland.

Each knows well the cost of practising the way of forgiveness. For one human being to forgive another a serious wrong means paying a high price in terms of foregoing your right to the old Mosaic Law of "an eye for an eye"; it means sinking your pride, not forgetting but setting aside the past, and trying to look with love at someone who appears to deserve only your anger and contempt. The cost is very often the Cross.

Sybil Phoenix has often found this in her concern to make people aware of the racism that still lies at the heart of British society, and Una O'Higgins O'Malley in her desire to bring those who are politically and religiously opposed to understand their common humanity, to listen to what each is saying, and to make some public act of penitence for the sins and hurts of the past. Both do so, not because either has a simplistic understanding of politics, but because each has faith in that powerful force for good which is evidenced in the actions of many individuals at times of outrage or disaster, and because each believes there can be such a concept as "the politics of forgiveness": that forgiveness (in Una Kroll's words) is "a valid political action, perhaps the most important political action open to Christians who know that we are taught by Christ to ask God to 'forgive us as we forgive those who trespass against us'."

Although we have seen in our own century powerful examples of the effect of non-violent action, we are only on the verge of understanding the politics of forgiveness as that applies to larger communities, whether in Brixton or in Belfast. I guess it will have something to do with unleashing those forces for good within us all (being made, as we are, in the image of God) which can happen when we make an act of forgiveness which is public and therefore courageous, and freely chosen and therefore joyful and liberating.

The whole weight of the Gospel lies in this word "forgiveness": God's forgiveness of us, and therefore our forgiveness of ourselves and of one another. The very centre of Jesus's teaching, in his parables and his actions, lies in this aspect of God's nature. But he doesn't only tell stories about God's forgiveness or demonstrate it in his relationships with the paralysed man or Mary Magdalene, or the woman taken in adultery; he lives it out in the most costly way possible as he is nailed to the Cross with the words, "Father, forgive them, for they know not what they do". With these words he takes us to the heart of the nature of Love (and therefore of God); further, he absolves his followers of any obligation to revenge his death, and makes plain by what principle they now have to act. The old law of retaliation is done away, the old corrosive chain of tit-for-tat, the bitterness from which there seems no escape, and a new, creative, life-giving way is revealed.

Let me match the two women who are centres of

hope in Brian Frost's book with the witness of two men.

During the Second World War the author Laurens van der Post found himself in a Japanese prison camp. In a book about his experiences (*Night of the New Moon*) he writes of the untold cruelties done by the Japanese guards to his fellow British prisoners. And then he writes this:

> It was amazing how often and how many of my men would confess to me, after some Japanese excess worse than usual, that for the first time in their lives they had realized the truth, and the dynamic liberating power, of Jesus' words from the Cross, "Father, forgive them, for they know not what they do". The tables of the spirit would be strangely and promptly turned, and we would find ourselves without self-pity of any kind, feeling deeply sorry for the Japanese as if we were the free men and they the prisoners . . .

My second experience is a familiar one from the same time, but some who read this may not know it and it is a most powerful witness to the exceptional power of forgiveness. When Leonard Wilson, the Bishop of Singapore, was captured by the Japanese he was put in prison in the notorious Changi jail where he was interrogated over a period of many months. For a while he suffered physical torture. After the war, with some reluctance, he spoke about that period of torture:

> In the middle of it they asked me if I still believed in God. When, by God's help, I said, "I do", they asked me why God did not save me, and by the

help of his Holy Spirit I said, "God does save me. He does not save me by freeing me from pain or punishment, but he saves me by giving me the spirit to bear it". And when they asked me why I did not curse them, I told them it was because I was a follower of Jesus Christ, who taught us that we are all brothers.

I did not like to use the words, "Father, forgive them", for it seemed too blasphemous to use our Lord's words, but I felt them, and I said, "Father, I know that these men are doing their duty. Help them to see that I am innocent." And when I muttered the words, "Father, forgive them", I wondered how far I was being dramatic and if I really meant it, because I looked at their faces as they stood around and took it in turn to flog me, and their faces were hard and cruel and some of them were evidently enjoying their cruelty. But by the grace of God I saw these men not as they were, but as they had been. Once they were little children playing with their brothers and sisters and happy in their parents' love, in those far-off days before they had been conditioned by their false nationalist ideals, and it is hard to hate little children.

But even that was not enough. There came into my mind, as I lay on the table, the words of that Communion hymn:

Look, Father, look on his anointed face,
And only look on us as found in him.
Look not on our misusings of thy grace,
Our prayer so languid, and our faith so dim;
For lo! between our sins and their reward
We set the Passion of thy son, our Lord.

And so I saw them, not as they were, not as they had been, but as they were capable of becoming, redeemed by the power of Christ, and I knew it was only common-sense to say "Forgive".

After the war, Bishop Leonard Wilson was to baptize and confirm one of the members of the Military Police who had flogged him. That is what is meant by redemption.

Looking at the Cross we are able to say: "Here is what we are capable of doing to each other, and to that which is of God in each other. Here is what we do to ourselves in our violent destructiveness. Here too is what we do to God. But we have a choice: what shall we do now?"

Many have understood that lesson and acted, even in times of great provocation and hurt, in a spirit of forgiveness. They are the true reconcilers, the true peace-makers. And this book is about just two of those who have lit candles in the darkness of our times.

MICHAEL MAYNE

Introduction

"Well, Polly, as far as one woman can forgive another, I forgive thee."

(John Gay, *The Beggar's Opera*)

When the Himalayan peasant meets the he-bear in
   his pride,
He shouts to scare the monster, who will often turn
   aside.
But the she-bear thus accosted rends the peasant
   tooth and nail
For the female of the species is more deadly than the
   male.

(*Rudyard Kipling*)

John Gay, writing in the eighteenth century, and Rudyard Kipling in the twentieth, knew that the female of any species defends her young with her life. In their defence she will be both cunning and aggressive, for so she must be if she is to fulfil her role in creation of securing the survival of her species. In that women have been and are no different from any other species, for throughout history they have fought on behalf of themselves and their children, endured hardships, survived wars, resisted genocide, sold their bodies to keep alive for their children, spied for their allies, scratched a living out of semi-desert, walked long miles to fetch water for their families. That kind of single-minded aggressiveness has led them sometimes to use men as weapons of self-defence, for they know that men are more expendable than themselves as far as the preservation of the species is concerned. There is, I believe a ruthlessness about women in certain spheres of human activity which makes them quite terrifying opponents in any situation of conflict, from a family quarrel to open warfare between nations. I believe this to be no less true of the stay-at-home, outwardly gentle and submissive wife than it is of the feminist activist, female spy or the enlisted woman who takes up arms in a guerrilla war. The one "uses" men to fight on her behalf and those of her young; the other considers that she is expendable, but still fights for the preservation of the species or for improvement in the lives of her children and succeeding generations.

The knowledge that females can be more aggressive than males in self-defence and defensive activities, that it is lionesses who kill for the pride, not lions, that she-bears will attack even in circumstances where males will turn and run, that Jael will kill Sisera without compunction rather than leaving Barak to catch up with him, has undoubtedly coloured our own attitudes towards female aggressiveness, and indirectly affected our attitudes towards women's abilities to forgive their enemies.

Men are afraid of women. They are afraid of women's capacity for aggressive defensiveness. Since men's physical strength is generally greater than that of women, and since men regard themselves as of major importance in generation, and are proud of their seminal role in the preservation of the species, they know it is in their own interests to dominate women and they do this not only by displays of physical strength but also by persuading women to behave unagressively. Women are exhorted to be "feminine", good, gentle, submissive, compassionate, and all-forgiving. One of the results of this need of men to tame women's aggressiveness has been the growth of belief that women are only true women if they conform to their role expectation. They are sometimes expected to conform to role models that are quite unrealistic, and when they cannot live up to those role models are portrayed as monstrous distortions of the female sex.

Women listen to these expectations and respond either by trying to conform or by being themselves. Some women undoubtedly still wish to conform to the role expectations set for them by men. In most affluent industrialized societies they are free to do so, although it should be remembered that in some women the quiet, unassuming, submissive behaviour may conceal an aggressiveness that only erupts when they discover that the security that male protection brought them is destructible, and they find that they cannot forgive the person or project that threatens to rob them of their hard-worked-for security. Other women refuse to conform to stereotyped feminine behaviour. They know that they have been released from the heavy physical burdens of repetitive motherhood and are therefore free to use their energies on behalf of species preservation in different ways. Among these women are those who are more outwardly aggressive than others. Some women find it easy to hate and to take their revenge: others prefer to forgive and forget, because they feel that is a more human way for both men and women to live. They would like to see men as well as women make peace not war in that way. I do not think that there is evidence to show that women are either more or less forgiving than men. I can find outstanding men, like Gordon Wilson of Enniskillen, whose daughter was killed in the Remembrance Day tragedy of 1987, who forgave the assassins at great cost to himself. I can match his witness by that of Una and Sybil. I listen often to Dag Hammarskjöld's comments in *Markings*, and I am equally attentive to St Teresa of Avila, whose writings on forgiveness are timely and timeless (*The Way of Perfection*, chapter 10). I can point to men and women whose capacity to forgive is very great, but equally to others who think of nothing but revenge. While I consider that men and women are equally forgiving, or unforgiving, I do think that there is some evidence to show that women remember grievances more clearly and with more detail than men, and that they tend to take longer to forget painful memories and to forgive those who have hurt or abused them. These traits may be the result of social conditioning but I tend to think that they are also genetically linked. I am not aware of research that is convincing in support of either view. What is known, however, is that in recent years women have been much more outspoken about their feelings, more active in society, and well to the fore in working for reconciliation in professional and public ways, for example, as Marriage Guidance counsellors or peace workers.

Many women who work for reconciliation between the sexes, races and nations do so because they feel that the human species can only survive and develop if men and women, people of different races and nations, learn to live in peace with each other and not at war. I do not personally view the last decade's emergence of women as leaders in various fields of reconciliation work as unusual in any way. Their involvement in peace work, for instance, is a natural use of their aggressive defensiveness for the sake of their children's future. With only few exceptions, women have always sought to preserve the lives of their children, but their liberation from serial pregnancies, together with greater availability of educational facilities have enabled them in recent years to take a more active political role in securing for future generations a nuclear-war-free future. I believe that we need the clear sightedness of women as well as that of men in this and other fields, and must rejoice in their articulate and emphatic pleas for the kind of reconciliation that can establish justice and peace in our world, by whatever means of disarmament possible, unilateral or multilateral. I also see the outspokenness and work of women in the fields of racism, classism and sexism in the same light.

One essential prerequisite for any kind of reconciling work between human beings is, I believe, an ability to forgive, by which I mean an ability not to act unjustly and hurtfully towards other people as they have acted towards you. Another is the ability to receive forgiveness.

Brian Frost has done us all a service, I believe, by writing about two people who have been called to forgive heroically. Una O'Higgins O'Malley is an Irish Catholic who "has Ireland's tragedy in her blood". Her father, Kevin O'Higgins, was the victim of political assassination on 10th July 1927. Before he died Kevin O'Higgins forgave his assassins and told his wife, "you must have no bitterness in your heart for them". Una, who had been born some six months before her father's death, grew up knowing that she was "bred in the nationalist tradition, whose great grandfather, grandfather, father and uncles were in turn jailed by British authorities", bred, therefore, into a tradition of political opposition to past and current British policies in Irish affairs. Those who grow up in such a tradition commonly find that their determination to secure justice is fuelled by anger, which is fed by individual and collective memories of past and present injustices. Una O'Higgins O'Malley acknowledges her roots; yet she works for peace, the kind of peace that demands justice but can only happen when people like her are willing to suffer for their belief that the way to peace lies through mutual forgiveness.

Sybil Phoenix, the other person portrayed in this study, is a Guyanan who came to Britain in 1956 and stayed to become a peace maker between those caught on both sides of the racial conflict. She is a community worker in South East London. In the course of her life Sybil Phoenix has had much to forgive, for she has suffered personally and also as a representative of other black people. She has admitted to "bitterness towards white people (for their racism), towards God (for the loss of a daughter) and fear of racial attacks" (see p. 77). Yet she believes that forgiveness is essential if people of different races are to live together in harmony. She understands the cost of that belief too, for it has sometimes made her unpopular with the very people she is trying to help, and she suffers deeply as she absorbs the bitterness of those on either side of the racial divide, and shares in Christ's pain which springs from his love for all his people.

These two women are convinced Christians: Una is a Roman Catholic; Sybil, a Methodist lay preacher.

Christ's teaching on forgiveness is central to their lives. They hear Jesus' words from the perspective of those who have much to forgive: "If any one strikes you on the right cheek, turn to him the other also" (Matthew 5:39); "Love your enemies and pray for those who persecute you" (Matthew 5:44); "Father, forgive them; for they know not what they do" (Luke 23:34).

Yes, here are two women who have suffered greatly and forgiven greatly: they are surely loved greatly by God. Yet in reading Brian's account of these two women I am aware of an additional factor that is necessary if the work of forgiveness is to bear fruit, and that is the forgiven person's, or group's, ability to receive forgiveness. Both Una and Sybil freely forgave those who had hurt them but there could be no true reconciliation unless and until that forgiveness was accepted. While in both cases some individuals have accepted their forgiveness, there is also evidence that others have found it harder to accept and have remained totally opposed to making peace of a kind that would last. There is a mystery here that needs a deeper analysis than I can provide, but I should nevertheless like to look at that essential prerequisite for reconciliation, the acceptance of forgiveness.

We can only begin to understand what being forgiven means, I believe, if we look at the relationship that is distorted by sin. When people do something they know to be wrong or hurtful to someone else, such as murdering someone's father, as happened to Una, or burning their precious club down, as happened to Sybil, they presumably want to make the victims suffer in order to exact retribution for things they know or imagine they have done to them. If innocent people, such as relatives or bystanders, suffer too, the avengers are indifferent to such suffering, for they can only see their own need for retribution or revenge. If they are unrepentant about their actions, or feel they are justified, then they will neither expect nor want to be forgiven either by God or by their fellow human beings. If they are caught by their fellow human beings and punished by society for their wrong doing they will neither expect nor welcome mercy. Indeed, they are likely to see mercy as a sign of weakness to be exploited in their own interests.

I have described the extreme reactions of some people who wreak vengeance on others. Relatively few people, however, start from that kind of position, but there must be, I think, a complex relationship between the murderer or arsonist and the victim which does not wholly absolve the victim of some responsibility. Indeed, in different ways both Una's story and Sybil's story show just a little of that relationship, for in different ways both women are distrusted and sometimes persecuted by the very people they identify with. Moreover oppressors and their victims are never isolated. Few of us are hardened sinners in our own families and communities, to the point where we actually commit murder or arson ourselves, but certainly we make those sins likely whenever we institutionalize and defend the sins of nationalism, racism, classism and sexism. The consequences of our individual and collective sins are that we become deaf and blind to the sufferings of those who are trapped by the social structures we erect to defend our own interests. We castigate those whose sins are sufficiently obvious to allow us to punish them properly, but we fail to notice how our own indifference and self-interests support the structures of injustice which provoke the revengeful or retributive action in the first place. I, who read these accounts of two heroic women and hear those same words of Christ's that they do, recognize that I am among those who need to be forgiven by them. I write as one who has in past times been indifferent to the sufferings of the Irish people, intolerant about their long memories and impatient with their apparent inability to compromise for the sake of each other. I write as one who, being white and affluent, has unconsciously oppressed those who are black and poor, whom, at one time, I presumptuously served in Africa and whom, at other times in England, I have self-consciously treated as equals. I also write as one who was tainted with classism and sexism, and needed to be converted from both. Can my experience, of changing from an unrepentant sinner to one who knows herself to be in need of forgiveness, help us to understand the mystery of repentance and acceptance of forgiveness in the work of reconciliation between human beings, who start from positions that are opposed to each other?

I have to say that in regard to sin of any kind very little change in me has ever been wrought by intellectual argument, education by others, persuasion or bribery. What changed my attitude was that I began to want to be forgiven when those whom I had consciously or unconsciously hurt let me know that they were hurt but refused to treat me as I had treated them. So long as I could not see what I was doing to them, or they did not show me their pain, I could escape from looking at the consequences of my actions. So long as I could pretend that I was right and they were wrong I could justify my sinfulness. So long as they pretended indifference to what I was

9

doing to them, or defiantly hit back, or threatened me with the same treatment as I had meted out to them, I remained impenitent. What changed me in regard to militant nationalism, racism, classism and sexism were the few people who dared to let me see their pain and who yet responded to me as if I could "put off your old nature" and "put on the new nature, created after the likeness of God in true righteousness and holiness" (Ephesians 4:22–23). Their visible suffering, together with their lack of desire to exact a penalty for the injustice they had suffered, and their appeal to the best side of my nature, helped the Holy Spirit to effect a change in me. That change was not completed in an instant, but it turned me in the right direction so that I could begin to listen to another viewpoint and find in myself the kind of thirst for justice that seeks true peace. Only then, I believe, could the Holy Spirit help me to work with God instead of against God. Nevertheless, it has been hard work accepting forgiveness. Sometimes I find myself remembering my past obtuseness in regard to particular people whom I have hurt, and being really surprised that they have apparently forgotten my sin and are not still feeling punitive towards me. I have also had to watch a tendency in me to expect, and therefore get, punishment. There is a perverse satisfaction in being punished for wrongdoing, and we human beings are sometimes unwilling to forgo that pleasure for the different pleasure that comes when we know that we are forgiven and restored to a relationship, as if we had not done the injury in the first place. Pride sometimes gets in the way of our accepting forgiveness, either from the hand of God or from our fellow human beings. So I know very well how difficult it is to accept that olive branch of peace that is offered. Those who offer it need to be very sensitive to the thinking and feelings of those who must receive it, if there is to be a true reconciliation between them. In dealing with stubborn men and women God is infinitely patient and humble, waiting graciously for us to accept what is on offer all the time through Christ's sacrificial love. In dealing with each other we need to look at the pattern given us by Christ and ask for help to accept forgiveness.

I have written about forgiveness from the perspective of someone who knows that she is a sinner in need of forgiveness. However, in the particular field of sexism I also have direct experience of being among those who need to learn to forgive. Most of that experience comes from being a woman in a Church and society where sexism is pervasive. It is in this field that I have experience akin to that of Una O'Higgins O'Malley and Sybil Phoenix, and so can identify with them in the belief that forgiveness is a valid political action, perhaps the most important political action open to those who are Christians who know that we are taught by Christ to ask God to "forgive us our sins as we forgive those who sin against us". As I learn, painfully, slowly, haltingly, to forgive my brothers and sisters who treat me and other women ignorantly and unjustly in a variety of ways, simply because we are women and for no other reason, I begin to feel awed by the mystery of the relationship between those who forgive and those who are forgiven, and come to a deeper understanding of our mutuality in Christ which helps me to listen to the history of these two women with fresh ears, and to keep going myself in the belief that reconciliation is both desirable and possible, and that it will be achieved with God's help – in God's own time.

UNA KROLL

Una O'Higgins O'Malley

Father – loving father of my enemy as well as of my friend – may your name be made holy throughout your marvellous creation. May we, your family, learn to do your will by loving and forgiving each other. Help us to realize that through love and forgiveness we can bring your heavenly kingdom into the here-and-now of the world you have given to us all. Supply us with the nourishment and the strength we need for this great task. Forgive us our apathy, our disbelief, our hopelessness, our greed, just as we forgive those who have neglected, taken advantage of, or sought to destroy us.

Do not allow us to deviate from this duty with which we have been entrusted; let us not doubt your support, your unfailing commitment to us, but guide us from the darkness of depression to the breakthrough of persevering hope.

We ask this, Father, through the merits of your Son, our brother, Jesus Christ; remembering his insistence that we love and forgive each other seventy times seven (as you also forgive us), we make our prayer to you in the knowledge that what is thus asked cannot be refused to us. Amen

To Editors of Main Newspapers

Sir,   19th March 1988
Defusing Terrorism

"Whatever Happened to the Red Brigade?" enquired Paddy Agnew in the *Irish Times* of 15th March 1988, who also has recently spoken on radio from Rome about the present state of that organization, ten years after the death of Aldo Moro.

He has told us how the widow of Moro's driver still holds out for vengeance against the terrorists who killed her husband but he has not, so far as I am aware, told how the families of Vittorio Bachelet (killed by the Red Brigade while Vice-President of the Italian Republic) and of many other victims made public acts of forgiveness.

In a piece entitled "Red Repentance" (*The Tablet* 24th October 1987) and also in the Jesuit Year Book of 1987, the work of Father Adolfo Bachelet, SJ (a brother of the assassinated Vice-President) is recorded. At the televised funeral of his father, a son of Vittorio Bachelet at once expressed the family's forgiveness. Three years later Father Bachelet, who had also expressed the same forgiveness, received a letter from prison signed by eighteen members of the Red Brigade. "We want you to come . . . We remember very well what your nephew said at his father's funeral . . . that ceremony when life triumphed over death and we, too, were overcome."

When life triumphed over death – by now Father Bachelet has continuing contact with up to two hundred former Red Brigade terrorists and remains in awe of the transformation in their lives and of the hope vibrant in them.

When life triumphed over death – we have felt it happen after Enniskillen and know that what Gordon Wilson expressed for like-minded people touched hearts in a unique way all round the world.

When life triumphed over death – I have personal knowledge of such a happening through the posthumous message of one of those who killed my father: "When he spoke to us of his forgiveness I felt all the anger flow out of me and my conscience could no longer hold out against him. Tell his family this."

Forgiveness is the strongest of all weapons available to man. Though we may not want to face up to using it, we *do* have a means of defusing terrorism, of overcoming death. At present we need to strengthen and extend links of forgiveness, so that they embrace this whole island.

UNA O'HIGGINS O'MALLEY

Una O'Higgins O'Malley's father, Kevin O'Higgins, was a member of the first independent Irish government of modern times. He had a subtle and fertile mind, with a crystal clarity about it. Devoted as he was to Irish independence ("One thing, and one thing only, has Ireland a right to from England," he once wrote, "and that is the recognition of her absolute independence"), he yet took a long view when the terms of the Treaty between Britain and Ireland contained less than he had hoped by way of a political settlement. Indeed, when De Valera indicated he would not accept the agreement, O'Higgins begged him on his knees not to cause a split. "He reminded him of the Parnell split and the ruin it brought to the Irish cause. 'It will', he said, 'be like releasing the West Wind' ".[1]

O'Higgins was always for taking the statesman-like approach and handling conflicts with measured consent. "I hardly hope that within the terms of this Treaty there lies the fulfilment of Ireland's destiny," he argued, "but I do hope and believe that with the disappearance of old passions and distrusts, fostered by centuries of persecution and desperate resistance, what remains may be won by agreement and by peaceful political evolution."[2]

Such was not to be the case, however, as civil government became impossible and disorder spread. Tragedy followed tragedy, engulfing Michael Collins, one of the Pro-Treaty leaders, himself. Kevin O'Higgins met the gunboat bringing back the body of Collins for burial. It was but ten days after the death of Arthur Griffith that Collins, on a tour of inspection, had been shot through the head in an ambush near his birthplace.[3]

On 10th July 1927, Kevin O'Higgins was to suffer the same fate as his father before him. His family had gone to church earlier, leaving him to go alone later. "At the corner, where Cross Avenue meets Booterstown Avenue, there was a seat," his biographer wrote, "and Mrs O'Higgins, on her way home from an earlier Mass, noticed, without attaching any

17

significance to the fact, that men were sitting there."[4] Kissing his wife and children goodbye he left for church without his bodyguard, even though he was Minister of Justice and External Affairs, and Vice-President of the Executive Council. A few minutes later revolver fire was heard coming from the road.

"O'Higgins was alive," his biographer continues, "but in dreadful agony. One bullet had entered the head behind the ear. Six were in his body."[5] He was able to speak, murmuring, "I forgive my murderers". Then, as he remembered the problem the Government would have without him, he said: "My colleagues! My poor colleagues!" Five hours later he was dead.

Una O'Higgins O'Malley thus had in her earliest life experience (she was almost six months old at the time of his death) both a political and a personal history with which to come to terms. Indeed, her grandfather's death had led his widow to call together all her sons to kneel around their father's remains and pray for forgiveness for those who had killed him. "People say I have a strong faith", she has observed. If it is true it certainly is rooted in those early years. "For me forgiveness was made easier because I had to handle it as a small child," she maintains about the core ingredient of her faith, "from when I was first aware of Christian teaching. I was very young, but I knew I could never assist at a Mass without including in it the people who had murdered my father." "I heard prayer defined recently as 'openness to God's love'," she added. "I like to feel I am reasonably open to God's love – it is a gift as a result of my father's forgiveness."[6] "I found it harder to forgive what had been done to my mother than to the father I had not known for long," she has added,[6] for Una's

18

mother, outgoing and charming, gave an impression of calmness and relaxation, but the effects of her husband's death left a heavy mark on her for the rest of her life.

Una's father "having taken the 'Pro-Treaty' side following the Anglo–Irish conflict of the years 1916–1922", writes Bishop Cahal Daly (the Bishop of Down and Conor) "was himself assassinated by a member of the 'anti-Treaty' side, being the section of the old IRA who rejected the Treaty of 1922 and were determined to continue the armed conflict."[7]

To understand the assassination in detail you have to go back to 1922. That year, on 22nd December, two Deputies were fired on as they left their hotel to attend the Dail. One died, the other was wounded. The Cabinet was called and the then Minister for Defence and the Army Representative in the Government asked that four Republicans, who were in custody, should be taken out and shot without trial, as a deterrent.

Eventually all the Executive Council agreed. The four men were leaders from the four provinces, in prison since the capture of the Four Courts. The Leinster victim was Rory O'Connor, who only a year before had been best man at O'Higgins' wedding.

Awakened from sleep, they were given till dawn to prepare themselves, then taken into the yard of Mountjoy Prison and shot. O'Higgins, Minister for Home Affairs, had to defend the decision. He justified it by arguing that it was not an act of revenge. "The members of the Parliament of Ireland must be kept free and safe to perform their duties", he maintained.[8]

The killings were to pursue O'Higgins until his death, especially the shooting of Rory O'Connor.

"One of the most blood-guilty Irishmen of our generation", *An Phoblacht* called O'Higgins.

It is an incident which has stayed with his daughter Una, too. Indeed in the 1970s she was writing:

> "For those who marvel that my father's daughter could advocate the need for politics of forgiveness when his years of office as first Minister for Justice were known as a firm law-and-order administration I would say: It is precisely because of the agonising dilemma of such office-holders as my father that I believe there is need for a politics of forgiveness. His dying words of forgiveness and of compassion for those who had killed him could only be expressed by the individual released from the burdens of his Office. What if he had survived the attack? For how much longer shall we be content to allow our society to function on these two different levels, to uphold one set of standards officially while individuals may respond quite differently to the challenges which face them? . . . . Moreover, apart from the testimony of Ernest Blythe that my father was the last but one of the Cabinet to agree to the executions of Irregulars in December '22, and that it had been very difficult to persuade him to give his consent, I think that any man, fortunate to live long enough, might reassess the effectiveness of certain measures in the light of subsequent developments."[9]

Kevin O'Higgins was an unusual man, not only in his dying words, but in his living, for at one point he was preparing to negotiate with the Northern Unionists (who by the Treaty of Settlement had a separate Parliament set up at Stormont in Belfast), suggesting to their former leader Lord Carson, then in retirement in London, a Dual Monarchy system (along the Hapsburg model) whereby the British King would be crowned King of Ireland in a separate ceremony.

Thus Una O'Higgins had in her family history three ingredients on which to draw in her public peace work which began in earnest in the 1970's: her father's act of forgiveness; the need to heal the wounds left by the Civil War in the south of Ireland; the need for some British/Irish reconciliation.

Recently (11th July 1987) a Memorial Mass was held at the Church of the Assumption, Booterstown, Dublin for O'Higgins *and* the three men who were said to have assassinated him. (No one has ever been apprehended for the shooting, but in a recent Memoir Mr Harry White, a Belfast Republican, recounts how the late Archie Doyle confided to him that he, along with Tom Coughlan and Bill Gannon, all now dead, had killed O'Higgins.)

"This divided island has much to repent and much to repair", Professor Enda McDonagh said at a concelebrated Mass arranged by Una, before a congregation which included the former Taoiseach, Dr Garret Fitzgerald, the Lord Mayor of Dublin and Dr Eamon de Valera, as well as two of Kevin O'Higgins' sisters. "The idea really originated with my father", Una observed. "As he was dying he said that he forgave his killers. We must be able to hold these Anniversary Masses with all included or we cannot do them at all." After the Mass a relative of one of his killers and Una greeted each other and talked privately.[10] Another phoned with the information that after O'Higgins had been shot he told the assassins that he forgave them, a fact not known till then.

> "The manner in which she has transcended all
> bitterness about her father's assassination", Dr
> Garret Fitzgerald has written, "has been out-
> standing, and the recent example of this was a
> quite breathtaking example of the imagination
> with which she pursued the concept of forgiveness
> in politics. . . . It is a measure of her standing
> that although there are many who would find
> it very difficult to emulate her, and although
> the reaction of some to her initially in regard
> to the Mass was sceptical, there was general
> acceptance of its genuineness and of its potential
> value."[11]

The irony of the history in which Una finds herself
involved is that Kevin O'Higgins was perceived,
"wrongly as it turned out", as the architect of the
reprisal policy of executions in the Civil War.[12] That
same sensitive approach which led her to organize the
Mass of Reconciliation Una showed in response to a
letter in *The Irish Times*, on 17th September 1984,
from Kevin Burke, Editor of the *Republican News*.
Here he had argued that the recent commemoration
of Michael Collins in County Cork by the Coalition
Minister for Justice, Michael Noonan, missed the
ruthlessness of the way Collins had pursued Irish
independence and the callous shootings which were
espoused at the time. What was now needed, Burke
argued, if his argument was correct, was a sustained
support for the IRA.

Una replied with one of her tightly packed letters
on 29th September:

Commenting on the response by the Editor of *An Phoblacht* (17th September) to the oration of the Minister for Justice at Beal na mBlath, Mary Blackwell asks (21st September) "What if the dream [of Collins] has failed?" and maintains "we cannot bear the reality". But since "Peace begins with me" how can we work and pray for lasting peace if, all the time, we are afraid to face the reality of our past? No work for peace is more painful than facing ourselves. *Can* we bear it?

As I understand it, there is reality in much of the window on the past opened by the Editor of *An Phoblacht*. The guerrilla war waged by Collins and his colleagues did manifest a dark and terrible side and whether we like it or not, it is on that and on the subsequent methods used by successive administration to contain anti-Government eruptions that our present State rests – as well as on the gallantry and statesmanship and self-sacrifice of our founding fathers commemorated by Mr Noonan at Beal na mBlath. This is our present *reality* – not a nightmare from which it is possible to awake. At some stage if we are to develop into a creative rather than a dependent nation ("Britain must do something", "The US must support a settlement", "The EEC must help us", etc) we are going to have to accept the past and handle more constructively its terrible consequences, some of which bedevil us today.

Within some context at present unthinkable this reality will have to be absorbed and treated by the then Government so as to bring about peace and justice (not simply law and order). Past virtues and values need not be betrayed but the whole will have to be assessed with openness.

Simultaneously the Republican Movement will have to discover a window on the *present* instead of forever looking backward to what it sees as the security of the past. Has Collins' dream of a United Ireland been achieved sixty years after? If not, have the successive IRA campaigns over the intervening years brought it any closer? Why have the great majority of Republican candidates been defeated so resoundingly when they have contested elections? Is not the Editor of *An Phoblacht* scoring an own goal when comparing the Provisional Movement with the first Sinn Fein, while not at the same time wondering why a United Ireland remains still only a dream?

Or is it that it is the journey itself (viz, the armed struggle) to which the Provisionals are really espoused, having lost the vision of any destination? (That armed struggle with its unspeakable brutalities.)

Anglo-Irish summits will come and go. Britain will be abjured to "*do* something", Unionists will be coaxed, terrorists deplored and, when possible, repressed. Meanwhile, we continue to build our prison together until such time as the issues raised by the Minister for Justice and the Editor of *An Phoblacht* are faced. If ever we are to have peace some day a healing will have to begin – cost what it may."

A Republican riposte drew another response from Una:

The logic of Thomas Doyle's letter (9th October) is at first appealing. Either we totally support the IRA or we banish further aspirations to unity.

Clear thinking, one might say, but does it meet our present situation?

The urgent task for us all in Ireland today is to make peace for people, between people, and people unfortunately tend not to fit within the rules of pure logic. Some Irish people want a 32-County Republic while others (in Ireland if not so "Irish") want a Northern "enclave". The armed Republican says to the latter, "If you cannot fit within my logic then my bullet and bomb will eliminate you". But I think Thomas Doyle's letter demonstrates that he himself would find this kind of logic worthless. Over half a century has passed since the deaths of Laim Mellowes and Erskine Childers but for him they have not been eliminated – (nor has Kevin O'Higgins for me). So, even if Republican ammunition were to destroy the "sectarian Northern enclave", would not its dead be a vivid source of motivation to their successors? How long could the 32-County Republic last in peace? There is a lot more to be done in preparing our future than applying simple logic.

As for our part, there is one binding strand stronger even than man-made weaponry which could, if we chose to use it, make us into the authors of our own destiny. I refer to the memorable forgiveness expressed by Erskine Childers and later by Kevin O'Higgins when facing death. "Calvary's great cry" of forgiveness can sustain our life while guns can only destroy. May Mr Doyle and all still suffering from the grief of the past experience its "Benison".[13]

Little did Una in her earlier life (she is married to a retired senior medical figure in Dublin, who himself comes from a prominent Fianna Fail family, and has six children and four grandchildren) imagine that in the 1970s her work would become as striking as it has. Even her use of two surnames, both of them redolent with southern Irish history, and her deliberate return to live in the house where her father died, show the context of her approach.

"It was the Northern Ireland situation, which erupted in the early 1970s," she has said, "which led me to become publicly involved."[14] She had read in a Dublin paper there was to be a picket outside the Sinn Fein HQ, indicating that if people felt they wanted to make a protest they should come along. "I carried a banner," Una recalls, "'You don't kill in my name'. Others had more stark banners, which surprised Sinn Fein officials, for they felt they were the true patriots."[15]

From that time some of the people kept together and in due course this led in Dublin to the formation of a group called *Working for Peace*. Its first activity was to organize holidays for mixed groups from both Protestant and Catholic communities in Northern Ireland.

Those organizing such activities felt a desire to do something to tackle the root cause of the violence in Northern Ireland. Soon it became clear that a radical change of attitude to people from different cultural and political traditions was needed, and towards the use of violence itself. A campaign was started to spread a message of non-violence and reconciliation to all Irish people.

The picket had been set up as a result of Bloody Friday, when Catholics had killed a number of Protestants, including the son of the Rev. Jo Parker, a Church of Ireland minister. He it was who set up a group *Witness for Peace* who kept vigil outside the City Hall in Belfast, with crosses for those who had died. Una went (as she has done continually) on one of her numerous visits to Belfast, this time to see the Rev. Ian Paisley and other leaders. These encounters, both then and since, have left her with an overall sense that at the root of almost any problem is pride. "The hardest thing any of us can do is to say we are wrong, to ask someone else's forgiveness", she has observed. "One set of people use their story in one set of terms. If you are trying to mediate and you are talking to them with any degree of compassion you do understand their situation. But I haven't yet come to know how to help get people off the hook. People themselves have to make some move to get off that hook."[16]

The movement for Peace of which Una was a part found concrete expression in the Glencree Reconciliation Centre in the Wicklow Hills outside Dublin. It was first opened in 1974, heralded by the first Annual Peace Week. Others followed, Una herself organising the 1981 Peace Week with a high degree of flair. Perhaps the most imaginative part was a Walk of Remembrance to areas associated with the Irish Civil War. Una was here again seeking to heal the memories of the South of Ireland's history. If there was to be a new future nothing could happen until the memories were healed, for often in Ireland there is no future, only the past happening over and over again in new guises.

The Report of the Peace Week succinctly describes what happened, below a picture of the leaders.

Several hundred people walked from St Patrick's Cathedral to the Four Courts on the quays and then to the GPO in O'Connell Street to remember Irish men and women – no matter to what tradition they belonged – who were killed by violence this century. The theme of the walk was one of forgiveness: "though they were divided in life, let us remember them together in death."

The walk was led by three prominent citizens carrying a shamrock of shamrocks – Nobel Prize Winner Sean MacBride, Peaceweek Chairperson Una O'Higgins O'Malley, and Irish actress Siobhan McKenna. At each point the shamrock was laid pausing to remember those who died in British forces, as a result of the Civil War in 1916, and in the bombs of 1974.

The event gained TV coverage on Irish TV, thereby contributing to many citizens' awareness of the need to heal the memories from past history.

Glencree started off as an attempt to found a Christian community seeing itself "as part of an emerging tradition of Christian communities dedicated to non-violence, a tradition which includes Taizé in France, Agape in Italy, Iona in Scotland, and of course Corrymeela in Northern Ireland". It accepted a Cross of Nails from Coventry Cathedral, and became one of its associated centres. Four Irish Church leaders together visited it and blessed a cross in a dedication service at Glencree.

However, the Christians who founded Glencree, among whom was Una, were very anxious not to exclude others (Christians not linked formally to a church, or non-Christians) as individual members, provided they were happy to be in association with a Christian community. Thus the individual did not have to attend worship, whilst accepting that the

28

community as such was committed to a Christian concept of reconciliation.

Built in to the foundation, therefore, was a difficult conception of co-operation, with no clear mechanism for resolving disputes if they arose. There was, therefore, both the potential for great creativity, yet also the possibility of unresolvable goals.

Inevitably such a Centre attracted both Christian and other idealists. Some saw it hopefully as an ecumenical counterpart to Corrymeela in Northern Ireland, which had strong Presbyterian roots. Others were perhaps more influenced by the Gandhian tradition, and were more aware of the contribution that conflict research made to the settling of disputes.

As time went on Una found herself involved in two major disagreements with the Centre. One was that there was no agreed way by which internal disputes, such as conflict within the community itself, could be mediated and the parties reconciled. She felt that as long as this problem of internal conflict was not faced and dealt with it was not easy to ask others to become reconciled. Another issue was the tension between the Christian and the non-Christian approaches. For a time, as Leader of Glencree, she found herself at the core of these problems, struggling to find a consensus to which members could adhere.

By the time Una was Leader the perceptions of Glencree were clearly not crystalline in the minds of many: was it primarily a Christian centre with a specific theology? Or reflecting the emerging debate about pluralism in the South of Ireland? What was its overall task? An early brochure described its aims thus:

To convince people (in both parts of Ireland and

elsewhere) that violence is destructive of the very ends it seeks to achieve, whether ideological, industrial or social;

To show people the moral strength of nonviolent action and what it can achieve;

To provide an opportunity for people to meet, talk and listen more easily and more honestly than is often normally possible;

To lend active support to non-violent movements trying to fight injustice and improve the quality of life in our society;

To provide a programme of peace education and research of international quality and value.

At no point in this particular brochure are the words "Christian" or "Christian community" mentioned. It is not surprising, therefore, with this contradiction in the dynamics, that there have been diverse interpretations of Glencree. Thus Peter McLachlan, a former assistant to the Northern Ireland Prime Minister, Brian Faulkner, has written of Una: "Her role in Glencree has always intrigued me. Glencree has suffered from never resolving its principal purpose – Christian or secular, political or educational. Una from the outset tried to give it a religious framework and purpose and in the end seems to have been rejected."[17]

The matter, as we have seen, was more complex. Moreover, in taking on Glencree maybe Una found herself involved in inter-group dynamics for which she had not been trained. If Glencree in some sense was a foretaste of a more pluralistic Ireland, with many sizes and shapes of people in it, a sharp mind was needed which could both interpret and guide such a pluralism. It might have been easier if Glencree had stayed with its pre-determined Christian position rather than moving into its later more fluid style.

Perhaps the conflicts which developed in the internal life of Glencree were inevitable. Moreover, though the Centre was ecumenical from the start (its first Chairman was a Methodist) inevitably in the South of Ireland ecumenical work had to be seen and organized in the context of a dominant tradition – that of the Roman Catholic Church. With such an overwhelming presence in the South this inevitably, as all large groups do, whatever their name, had an effect on how people acted and reacted. Glencree was perhaps just as vulnerable to the majority/minority problems of Ireland as elsewhere. Eventually, whatever the precise reasons for the conflicts, Una felt she could not go all the way with Glencree, and so resigned her post as Leader.

"I suppose", John Morrow, leader of Corrymeela, has commented, "she is a bit of an individualist and has sometimes found it difficult and frustrating to work with others in a team because she had a passionate belief in the need to take certain actions."[18]

Perhaps what happened over Glencree points to a weakness in prophetic witness: it tends both to sit lightly to structures and to be uneasy with all their complexities. And Una, for all her sharp political antennae (especially the value of symbolism in politics), and her awareness that there is a chemistry about forgiveness (a comment Dr J.A. Robb has made of her),[19] has, as often Father Brian Lennon has observed, tended "to see things in terms of individuals rather than of groups and classes, and sometimes, in my view, looks for reconciliation without some of the necessary structural changes that are required. That

31

is the kind of issue that she and I would have long arguments about."[20]

Essentially, of course, a prophetic role is to warn people of a situation in all its stark reality. It is this, rather than leading a group, with its need of consensus and ambiguity, which Una does so well, by an instinct rather than by argued reflection, though her intuitive mind can be penetrating. This is particularly true when it comes to the many facets of the Irish problem, for she has always been able to hold on to its many dimensions – the British/Irish, the North/South, as well as the Roman Catholic/Protestant conflict within Northern Ireland itself.

Una herself modestly maintains, "I have no credibility in politics".[21] Yet she does have an influence, even if it is an elusive one. Once, indeed, she stood for the Dail as an Independent, drawing 9 per cent of the vote, not enough to give her a seat under the arrangements prevailing at the time.

What brought her to stand against the then Taoiseach was her feeling that if there was to be peace, justice would have to be seen to be done, and the Garda (the police in the Republic of Ireland) were at that time not living up to the principle of the Founding Fathers. A combination of the issues of the Peace Movement, and her father's pride in the Garda (unarmed police serving impartially, no matter who was in government) drew her to respond to the criticisms (raised by *The Irish Times*) that the police were below the mark in some of their actions.

About one hundred people worked on her campaign, on a broad human rights and justice canvas. Liam Cosgrave's father had been the man under whom Una's father had served, so it was poignant that she was standing in the Prime Minister's constituency.

There was disappointment, too, that she had to stand up in public and to criticize her father's party, Fine Gael. But she was as usual willing to stick her neck out for *truth* as she saw it. As she was the only woman among the ten candidates she gained a high profile. "You cannot call other people to renounce violence," she argued, "until your own house is in order. It is no good telling the North of their wrong if you are not straight."[22]

Una's work vis-à-vis Northern Ireland is persistent, compassionate and always involved with people at the centre of the suffering there. "From where I'm based," she has observed, "the Unionists are a minority people in the whole of Ireland and need special study and consideration from Southern Catholics – a challenge for us to understand, one major challenge to our Christianity. It is nonsense to profess Christianity in the South and be unconcerned about the plight of northern Unionists."[23]

"All the sturdy independence of Northern Irish people cannot hide their innate helplessness and dependence on our assistance", she declared in one of her talks to an English audience. "Sectarian violence in Ulster has erupted in every century since the 'plantations' of the 1660s, so that present day Ulster people bear a burden of history which *somehow* has to be lifted from them. Added to that the terms of the partition of Ireland in the 1920s left them with an inevitable and sure recipe for disaster – a double-minority problem with approximately sixty per cent Unionists, people owing allegiance to this other island (strangely referred to as 'mainland Britain') and forty per cent aspiring to unity with the rest of Ireland, whose proximity causes the Unionists, though numerically a majority, to feel beleaguered and defensive as do minority people. Two sets of minority people then feel threatened and insecure with their joint heritage of violence . . .

"It seems to me," she concluded, "that it is on us, the British and the people of the Republic, the other sides of this eternal Anglo-Irish triangle – on us the less handicapped, as it were, that the major responsibility lies to bring Christ more fully to bear on this cruel conflict."[24]

This perception does not stop Una from forging her strong links with the North of Ireland, of course. Whether it is a private papal audience in Rome with a close friend from the Unionist community (to try to help Pope John Paul the Second understand Unionists' fears more directly by meeting one firm Unionist), or her collaboration with others from the South (and from Northern Ireland, too) in the *Faith and Politics Group*, Una seizes opportunities as they come. That group (for a long while Una was the only woman member) has produced some striking documents – *Breaking Down the Enmity*, *Understanding the Signs of the Times*, and *Towards An Island that Works*.[25]

Una's passionate involvement in groups like this one is what is often remembered most about her. What is perhaps less perceived is her diffidence, until she is drawn out by someone who encourages her to speak her mind. "She often found herself, I think, in a position of having an intuition which she found difficult to justify on rational grounds", Father Brian Lennon has observed. "At first, in many instances, the majority of the committee would reject her insights. However her persistence often won through and the value of her insights gradually emerged."[26]

The emphasis on *fear* in the first document is

something of which she is intensely aware, seeing its bondage. "In this complexity of fears," she has argued about Ireland, "this tangle of pride, is there no hope at all, no light in the darkness? Strange as it may seem the hope, the light *is* there where it has always been – right at the heart of the Good News of the Christian Gospel."

What is this Good News? "It is the vital question of forgiveness (vital in the sense of lifegiving) which underpins the whole of Christ's message. Indeed, we cannot pray to his Father unless we are at least trying to forgive . . . Trying Christianity in the Irish connection today," she continues, "would necessitate quite a few headaches! Doing what we would have them do to us would have Unionists rushing to insist on power-sharing, while Nationalists, especially the Southern ones, would hardly wait to expunge their claims to unity, since these cause Unionists to feel threatened. In Britain the Christian response would ensure that the Northern Ireland agony would be given top priority to its deliberations. In the US – Irish-Americans . . . would hasten to remove press- ure for anything except better understanding and peace in Ireland."[27]

In a sense Una is grateful to be living in Ireland, for its crisis means that people can, if they wish, cut through "swathes of self-deception". As a leading Northern peaceworker insists: "It is the paramilitary inside myself that has, all the time, to be dealt with while simultaneously I try to help restrain the violence of others."[28]

Una spares no truth, however, though it is always wrapped in words chosen deliberately both with skill and sensitivity in order to get movement from different groups. Thus, addressing a Corrymeela

35

Community meeting in Coleraine, she has argued that the Loyalist has the problem more in his hands "and it is with him the greater potential for peace lies". "Was there not, under Gladstone, a consensus (or at all events a near-consensus) of the people of these islands favouring Home Rule for Ireland and a re-creation of an Irish identity and vitality which had sadly collapsed after the Act of Union in 1800 and the cessation of Grattan's Parliament? And was it not a tiny minority of the people of these two islands, viz. the Ulster Loyalists, who so resisted that development that Gladstone's nineteenth century vision of an Anglo-Irish reconciliation had to be abandoned?"

She went on to argue that twice more – once in the second decade of the twentieth century, and once in the 1970s, at the collapse of the Sunningdale Agreement, with its proposal for a power-sharing Executive – the Ulster Loyalists showed themselves unable to work with any compromise. The South, however, she felt, had now reached some form of compromise over its original aspiration of a 32-County Ireland, some form of federal, or confederal, arrangement being acceptable.

It was because the Hillsborough Agreement, signed by the then Taoiseach, Dr Garret Fitzgerald, and Mrs Margaret Thatcher, in November 1985, brought the possibility of a change in relationships that Una welcomed it, although acknowledging with her usual realism that it was far from what she had hoped might be forthcoming. She took Conor Cruise O'Brien to task in an Open Letter for his negative attitude to the historic Agreement between Britain and the Republic of Ireland. "I breathe more freely," she wrote, "because our government has formally recognized

Britain's role in the North, also that the Unionist position is once more endorsed by the British. I am delighted that the special identity of Northern nationalists is recognized for what it is, and that structures are provided to maintain this recognition. We could find common cause in dismay that Unionists were not consulted about the Agreement but since, to the best of my recollection, 'Ulster' has been given to saying very little but 'No', I can't say I am very surprised by this."

"I am not saying", she summed up, "that Hillsborough is perfect, nor even that it 'will work'. I am saying that it contains potential for development of trust between those sorely divided – if they had a mind to work it." She urged him, therefore, to encourage people to make the Agreement work rather than to be negative and pessimistic.[29]

Una again returned to the theme in June 1986, at a public rally in Dublin organized by Glencree, and subsequently published in *Doctrine and Life*. "It is devastating to realise," she ended, "that Ireland in the eighties is imprisoned by the same absolutes as in the early decades of this century." Despite all the horrors since – two world wars, Hiroshima, drug-abuse and widespread unemployment "neither singly nor together have such reminders of mankind's frailty and essential inter-dependence distracted us from the eternal question of sovereignty over the twin steeples of Fermanagh, Tyrone and their neighbouring counties."[30]

Essentially Una saw the Hillsborough Agreement in terms of forgiveness and reconciliation. The result of the South being able to forgive Britain her previous role in Ireland was to acknowledge Britain's involvement in the North. The result of Britain's recognition that there were two traditions present in Northern Ireland – the Nationalist and the Unionist – was a willingness to work with the South over Northern Irish issues *and* a firm guarantee to the Unionists that their security and their identity were acknowledged. Una's Press Release in April 1986 explained where she stood on the purity of Irish Nationalist claims to the whole of Ireland. "As one who has participated in the cross-border movement of peace and reconciliation for the past sixteen years, I urge southern people," she stated, "to examine Articles 2 and 3 of our Constitution in the new light of the preamble to the Anglo-Irish Agreement. Northern Unionists have rejected the Agreement in no uncertain manner. Is not much of their rejection caused by their belief that the Agreement is a back-door to a United Ireland? By rephrasing Articles 2 and 3 of our constitution we might be understood to be trying to live by the spirit of the Hillsborough Preamble." (The Preamble recognized and reaffirmed the need for developing reconciliation and neighbourliness between the British and Irish people in their unique relationship.)

Una hoped that the South, as perhaps its elections demonstrated, had absorbed the Anglo-Irish Agreement and did not want it re-negotiated. Most hoped that some form of devolved government for the North could be worked out which could bring peace and stability. Yet, she felt, too, both Republicanism and Unionism were continuing faithfully "to mirror each other – at least in their stubbornness."

Mainstream opinion, on the other hand, she felt, did not harbour predatory intentions about the North and "where the question of unity is concerned realism prevails. What anti-British feeling remains seems to manifest itself only in response to some unusually lamentable happening in the North – such as Bloody Sunday in Derry or the deaths of the young hunger strikers."

There was still the issue of the complexity of religious problems and these would have to be addressed at some time if Ireland was ever to have peace. This sensitivity to the relation of religion to politics has been another of Una's contributions to reconciliation work in Ireland, as she seeks to allow a chemistry of forgiveness to alter the relations between the diverse religious traditions for how often in the past they have behaved to one another. Whether it has been the ecumenical service she organized at the time of the Pope's visit to the Republic, or her visits to speak at gatherings in England (she shared a platform at Great St Mary's, Cambridge with the Rev. Dr Ray Davey, the founder of Corrymeela), Una has grown in ecumenical awareness. "Her ecumenical involvements have made her self-critical," John Morrow has observed, "but also even more a deeply committed Catholic and I think her faith has deepened over the years."[31]

Briefne Walker, a priest with the Holy Ghost fathers in Dublin, senses a similar commitment. "Her personal and family history", he has written, "have led her to struggle with the divisions and many ambiguities of Irish history: the appalling record of the colonial past, blighted relationships between Ireland and Britain, and within Ireland, north and south. As I know her, Una O'Malley has struggled with the great Christian concepts of peace, justice, reconciliation. She has achieved a very personal vision of a reconciled society in Ireland.

"At the same time she is the very opposite of

a liberal 'do-gooder', untouched by the pain and the ferocious anger of violent conflicts. One of her strengths, I feel, is her capacity to make the imaginative effort to experience reality as 'the other side' sees it, especially when the instinct and views of the other are quite alien to one's own."[32]

It is perhaps her reaching out to Britain, revealing her capacity to forgive Britain's role in Ireland, which shows her sensitivity at its best. The writer was once involved in a seminar at Corrymeela and on the Sunday morning (it was Remembrance Sunday) there was an act of worship specially created for the occasion. As we prayed in the silence the voice of Una came loud and clear praying that the dove of peace might bear a poppy in her olive branch.

Similarly she engaged in a controversy over the observance of Remembrance Sunday, always a bone of contention in the South, which was officially neutral in the Second World War.

"Perhaps Comdt Jim Lavery and his group have forgotten", she began, "the thousands of Irishmen who died in the British forces; the many families who gave sons both to the British forces and to Sinn Fein; the many returned from British forces who subsequently joined the Irish Army in its early days; the numerous ways in which our citizens depend on air-sea rescue help from British personnel? Harrassment by British forces in Nationalist areas of Northern Ireland may, at times, be highly reprehensible, but forgiveness and honouring the dead can enlarge and ennoble our vision. Certainly, the nephew of Michael Collins and retired Chief-of-Staff of our Army, Lt-General Sean Collins-Powell, believed that when, during a walk of remembrance last Peace Week, he laid a wreath of shamrocks at the British memorial in St Patricks's Cathedral.

The then leader of Ogra Fianna Fail – Sean O'Connor, a grandson of Sean Lemmass – thought similarly and accompanied General Collins Powell, as did the Chairman of Young Fine Gael. Later, these two young men together laid wreaths at the Civil War focal point – the Four Courts – as a witness of Young Fianna Fail and Young Fine Gael to bind wounds. Could not Comdt Lavery and his comrades help this new spirit of co-operation and forgiveness?"[33]

Una's talk to the Social Studies Conference during her time as President of the Irish Association for Cultural, Economic and Social Relations, made two headlines – "We let the Provos do 'dirty work' for us: claim." And "Irish need Bob's [Geldof] spirit." There could not have been two more contrasting headlines from the same speech. Speaking as one "bred in the nationalist tradition, whose great-grandfather, grandfather, father and uncles were in turn jailed by British authorities", Una claimed that her understanding of Anglo/Irish relations (the topic of her address) was based on "loyalty to that past, not on rejection of it".

"Is it morally justifiable", she asked, "to identify Britain as the scapegoat without *some* realization of *why* Unionists cling to her so desperately?" Much work needed to be done – indeed, only the South of Ireland could solve the problem. "The dream of future unity which I cherish . . . will not be realized," she maintained, "within this century at least, because it is a dream in which people are in no way acting

41

out of pressure, from coercion, but unite together because it seems best to them that way. People like us in the South, from a tradition which has been at the receiving end of pride and aggression through the years, should surely be the last to try to dominate others?" It is we, if we do so, she continued, who are the life-blood of Paisleyism, his best support group. "Political Protestantism depends on our claims, our dreams, for its very existence. Without them it has no cause, no purpose, and Northern politicians would be left to deal with bread and butter politics of ordinary living." Moreover, she argued, "if Britain were to depart before we have won the confidence of Unionists, Ireland's state would be worse than at present." Britain, too, must be part of the reconciliation before our dream is fully realized. "We must become masters of our own destiny", she concluded.[34]

"Could it be," she had asked earlier in another context, "we have now come of age, realizing our independent worth as a nation and that, from now on, we may be capable of action from a positive and mature base rather than of re-action against deprivation and injustice. . . . Are we then at last a happy people – no longer insistent on past wrongs but capable of looking around us to recognize the good in others who have sinned against us in the past but against whom we have also sinned. Has Britain supported any of our emigrants or given us anything good apart from the wrongs which we all can detail?"[35] The debate "Northern Ireland – What Future?", included a number of prominent politicians. Once more Una demonstrated her capacity to mix with and doubtless influence opinion-formers with her own special insights and approaches.

42

Una's work is always rooted, of course, in her Christian conviction as she pleads for a politics of forgiveness. The task is in one way simple: "How to relate the Gospel of love and forgiveness which most of us are proud to inherit with politics's working of it?"[36] At the same time Una seems to be able to recognize that "the whole thing of forgiveness is immensely complex. I cannot be at all sure, for example, that even if the Irish were to say to the English that the Penal Laws etc., are now forgiven, this would not make matters much worse. The English might very well retort, 'But what about your acts of revenge, your present day bombings, etc.,' and things would get *worse* from then perhaps? But if one or other side was to *ask* for forgiveness the things might well progress from there?"[37]

"If I weren't taught by Christ to forgive," she has reflected, "would I forgive? The centrality of forgiveness is Christian. I'd like to feel I'd be forgiving as a person, a forgiving part of the fabric of the universe, but it took Christ to highlight the forgiveness of God.

"When I say as a Christian I have no option, it doesn't mean others are less forgiving – many who do not believe in Christ could teach many Christians about forgiveness."[38]

Surprisingly, when considering the contours of forgiveness, Una considers it may be easier to forgive a very big injury than comparatively minor ones, especially as one may not recognize the lack of forgiveness in more mundane matters. But a big event "brings you up to need to face that forgivingly or else be corroded by one's own refusal to forgive."[39]

Una's quality of forgiveness is all bound up with her own suffering. Her Christianity and her father's

43

political role, as we saw, have made it difficult to dodge this. From time to time she has met strong and active Republicans from many backgrounds, and they have conveyed to her "there was something in my listening to which they could relate because I *had* suffered – there was an authenticity in my concern. People who knew the price of bereavement can sense my own bereavement. Ian Paisley was the same.

"This was also true of the Provos with whom I had any meetings. I imagined people would feel antagonistic to me because of the executions but this was not so."[40]

When Una had these meetings some of her friends felt she went too far. "I spoke at one big meeting in the Mansion House," she remembers, "when they had five demands for the Hunger Strikers and said I could agree with four. There were hardly any others than Provo supporters at the meeting as it happened.

"You have to go as far as you can in both directions", Una considers. "I hated doing it because there was something in the whole Provisional meeting which appalled me, and to which I was allergic. Yet I took the initiative to attend."[41]

For all her capacity to move from one group to another to listen, Una still considers that when it comes to reconciliation she knows "as little as I did when I started trying to reconcile." Forgiving, which brings reconciliation, seems to relate, however, to the degrees a person has suffered. It is internal to oneself, and outwardly involves endlessly listening to two sides of a story, hoping one set of people might have a glimmer of what others are about. It is without doubt wearing. "It is not for nothing," Una observes drily, "the Cross is shaped as it is and the hands stretched out. People are literally pulled apart

44

if they really try to reconcile."[42]

Without doubt her unflagging attempt to link forgiveness and reconciliation, and, more importantly, her living of forgiveness, has had an effect in Ireland, though difficult to estimate. The work she has done to bring together people from different traditions because they trust her "has been much appreciated by those of us involved in politics who could not ourselves undertake this kind of activity", Dr Garret Fitzgerald has commented.[43]

"Last year in Zimbabwe . . . and after the European war . . . people came together and said 'If I forgive you, will you forgive me?' and made a way forward out of mutual forgiveness", Una maintained, as she tried to put her theology in popular terms in a radio interview. "I don't think in Ireland we have yet realized that forgiveness is a very powerful dynamic. But if we could approach Anglo/Irish relations in a spirit of mutual forgiveness and lift ourselves out of the centuries-old dilemma of all the wrongs that were done to us (and undoubtedly they were), I think we would be looking at peace and reconciliation and justice in a way that is constructive."[44]

Una's discipleship always has in it this reflective and courageous edge, which is theological and political. Commenting on a paper by Father Desmond Wilson she has made a remark which powerfully shows this, as she indicates she finds "the most important contribution is his assessment of Christ's prayer for forgiveness, in particular *the release of his followers by this from any obligation to avenge him.*"[45] "Sometimes I think," she concluded, "Christians should have invented the politics of forgiveness because that is what their faith is about. But they didn't. Will they?"

In similar vein, as she contemplates the fact that forgiveness can be a way to change the unchangeable, she has reflected: "It seems to me that this is mysteriously true but that the trouble is its truth cannot be experienced without making first a blind leap in the dark. *Who will first leap*? This is where all conflict sticks and where individuals stick unless they take the view, as expressed by Maximilian Kolbe, that reconciliation is a daily task of becoming internally reconciled to the good in oneself – rather than to the evil."[46]

As she wrestles reflectively she tries to work her convictions out in public life. Thus, as she ponders the depths of meaning in the word forgiveness, she will write: "I had an hour recently with one of the Provo leaders and put to him this idea of forgiveness being central to the true liberation struggle. I think this dynamic could and should be much developed where the Provos are concerned. Where the Loyalists are concerned I think much development of the ongoing effect of Christ's prayer for forgiveness is needed. Society in the North – certainly among the Northern majority – is, like many other societies, but even *more* so, based on ideas of law and order and retribution, etc. The fact that Christ's followers have been *freed* from obligations of revenge has not found root."[47]

In Una's view society needs convincing that the idea of linking forgiveness with politics is compatible. Secondly, to connect this with other words "more habitually associated with politics (such as 'enlightened', 'wise', 'statesmanlike', 'magnanimous'). The Hillsborough Agreement is a 'forgiving' thing as compared with traditional Southern green nationalism, but the *word* 'forgiveness' might cause mayhem

both among Northern nationalists *and* British Unionists."

A third stage is needed, too, Una feels: "It is the
point at which the interconnection of the other words
and forgiveness is pointed out, and it is shown how
forgiveness underlies most human affairs."[48]

Una returns ultimately again and again to the
gospels, as she concludes, "Unfortunately Christ
is simply not available for the highlighting of our
antagonisms, the consolidation of our divisions. The
only way in which he is available to us is on his own
terms of brotherhood and forgiveness – brotherhood
with, and forgiveness of, our enemies. Tough – but
true, and really it is hard to see how he could have
made his terms much plainer. 'Must I really forgive
my brother seven times?' 'No – seventy times seven.'

"But, of course, we will not have it so. Even
the mystic Pearse – perhaps especially the mystical
Pearse – for all his poetic insights and religious
preoccupation with the blood sacrifice of Calvary
was, alas, himself the fool to boast of 'our Fenian
dead' at the culmination of a Christian burial service.
Because, of course, in Christ there *are* no Fenians, or
Loyalists, nothing but one body, one Spirit."[49]

"More than anyone else in Ireland, I believe,"
Breifne Walker has written, "Una O'Malley has
conveyed one message very clearly in the course
of her life: if the historic goals of Irish nationalism
are to be realized, our remembering of the past must
be in the service of the truth about that past, and in
the service of forgiveness. Contemporary nationalist
politics must make room for forgiveness; only in this
way can we have justice in our relationships."[50]

"For me," writes the Irish journalist Louis McRedmond, "she personifies Christian forgiveness."[51] It

the kind of comment which makes Una O'Higgins O'Malley smile wryly, for she and her family know how often she has to struggle to follow the way of Christ.

Notes: Una O'Higgins O'Malley

1. *Kevin O'Higgins*, Terence de Vere White (Methuen and Co Ltd 1948) p. 65
2. Ibid p. 75
3. Ibid p. 103
4. Ibid p. 240
5. Ibid
6. Interview with author
7. Bishop Cahal Daly, letter to author, 4th September 1987
8. Dail Reports No 2, p. 67
9. Una O'Higgins O'Malley, "Why a politics of forgiveness?" From Section 1, *Forgiveness and Politics – Britain and Ireland A Test Case?* (Forgiveness and Politics Study Project, 1984)
10. *Irish Times*, 13th July 1987
11. Dr Garret Fitzgerald, letter to author, 10th September 1987
12. *Irish Times*, 13th July 1987
13. *Irish Times*, 17th October 1984
14. Interview with author
15. Ditto
16. Ditto
17. Letter to author, 28th September 1987
18. Letter to author, 26th August 1987
19. Letter to author, 17th September 1987
20. Letter to author, 28th September 1987
21. Interview with author

22. Ditto
23. Ditto
24. Una O'Higgins O'Malley from a talk given at a Vigil for Reconciliation in Northern Ireland at East Hendred, Berkshire, 11th October 1980
25. *Breaking Down the Enmity* and *Understanding the Signs of the Times* can be found in *Choose Life* (Christian Responses to the Northern Ireland Conflict) and have been published by An Inter-Church Group on Faith and Politics. (8, Upper Crescent, Belfast, BT 7, Northern Ireland). *Towards an Island That Works* (Facing Divisions in Ireland) may also be obtained from there or from 169, Booterstown Avenue, Co. Dublin, Republic of Ireland.
26. Letter to author, 28th September 1987
27. Una O'Higgins O'Malley, "The Bondage of Fear", November 1983
28. Letter to author
29. Published in an article in *The Irish Times*, January 1986
30. Una O'Higgins O'Malley, "Doctrine and Life" (Dominican Publications September 1986)
31. Letter to author, 26th August 1987
32. Letter to author, 8th September 1987
33. Letter to *Irish Press*, 31st October 1983
34. Social Studies Conference, August 1985
35. Talk at Literary and Debating Society, "Northern Ireland – What Future?", October 17th 1979
36. Letter to *The Irish Times*, 14th June 1978
37. Letter to author
38. Letter to author
39. Interview with author
40. Letter to author

41. Letter to author
42. Interview with author
43. Letter to author, 10th September 1987
44. Interview on RTE, 18th May 1981
45. Letter to author
46. Letter to author
47. Letter to author
48. Letter to author
49. Una O'Higgins O'Malley, "De Mortuis" in *The Furrow* – News and Views, Autumn 1987
50. Letter to author, 8th September 1987
51. Louis McRedmond, letter to author, 8th October 1987

Sybil Phoenix

Change is painful and costly
As grace is not cheap

Father God, I thank you for this new day.

Forgive me for all the pain I caused you and others
yesterday

Through what was done to me by my friends and
neighbours.

The hurt just would not go away.

I pray you, Father, change me and enable me to
forgive.

Take away the pain and put a loving spirit in me.

Father, I trust you through the Victory and the power
of the Cross,

its length, its breadth, its height, its depth.

As you gave yourself to gain my soul, change me into
a forgiving person and set me free to love all my
neighbours and friends.

Widen my vision not just to stay on the mountain top,
but

Jesus, as you took your disciples down to ground level
to

see other visions, help me to face the issues before me.

Strengthen me in power, give me your inward peace,
for I am thine,

O Father.

I know you can make me whole again through your
love for me.

Amen.

It hurts too much to hate. Hating is a burden to me. For me to survive and to be useful to myself and to the community I serve I find it easier to forgive.

You may dislike what someone, or the community, does to you. But I cannot cope with hating, even though I get angry with what is done to me.

But in the end I find it easier to discover ways of forgiving a person what they have done to me than to continue to hold something against them.

Because of that I get into hot water. People condemn me – yet I find it difficult to be other people's judge and jury. You see, because of my own sin, I see how easy it is to do wrong things. All the time I am assessing what I do; how much wrong I am committing, how faithful I am being.

Because I am a follower of Him who said, "The person who is without sin cast the first stone", I try to live by forgiveness.

Sybil Phoenix (in an interview, Spring, 1988)

Sybil Phoenix's history is radically different from Una's secure and stable middle-class home and environment in Dublin. Sybil was born in British Guiana (now Guyana) the year Una's father was assassinated. Her mother died when she was ten, and Sybil moved in to live with the family of her grandfather. When she was twelve her grandfather died, and she moved again – this time to live with an uncle and aunt. "As I had no mother or father to turn to and was brought up by other people," she has said, "I always *felt* the loss of parents to love me."[1] (Sybil's father remarried shortly after his wife's death and more or less deserted Sybil and her brothers.)

Very soon Sybil's Christian convictions became apparent when she demanded of her grandfather that she become a full member of the African Methodist Episcopal Zion Church, where the family worshipped. Sybil got her way, telling her grandfather that he was behaving as badly as Jesus's disciples when they stopped children approaching Jesus (Mark 10:13–16).

When Sybil went to live with her aunt life was difficult as they did not get on. Apparently her aunt had not got on very well with her sister, Sybil's mother, and Sybil was treated as a servant.

Mrs Lynch, the aunt, was very black, whereas Sybil's mother had been fair-skinned. Although the sisters had the same parents their colour was different because their great-grandmother had been white, originally from Scotland. Travelling to British Guiana to live with her brother, she had met and married an African who had settled in Guiana after he had deserted from the Boer War in South Africa. Thus colour was a factor early in Sybil's perceptions of the world, as she experienced her aunt's jealousy of her sister. (In the West Indies fairer-skinned people like Sybil's mother could get better jobs and earn a more adequate salary than others.)

As a child Sybil loved singing and belonged to a choir at the YWCA. One day, when Sybil was about fourteen, the woman who ran the British Guiana Philharmonic Choir heard Sybil sing "O Danny Boy", and offered her a place in the choir, usually only comprising white Americans and English people.

While still at school Sybil helped in a youth club, and when at sixteen she left school she became secretary to the minister at the church. On top of this, in order to earn extra money, she returned to the school as a part-time teacher of domestic science and dressmaking. She also took a three-year evening-class course to become a social worker, afterwards visiting church members and others who needed help. Her social work experience was immediately put to use in the youth club, which by now she was running.

Sybil met Joe Phoenix, her future husband, when he came to join the club. He worked for a stationer's in Georgetown and was responsible for importing paper and books for his firm.

At the age of twenty-two Sybil planned to earn her living as a professional seamstress amd hat-maker, so she bought two sewing-machines and with Joe set up a firm. Joe's role was to take the things Sybil made and, using his business contacts, find places where he could sell the dresses and hats. They did well and their business prospered.[2]

In 1956 they decided they wanted to see something of the world beyond British Guiana, and set off to visit England, arriving by boat at Portsmouth. Their visit was to be both an adventure holiday and also a time to get some more training for work they were planning to do when they returned home.

Events did not turn out like that, however, for Britain fascinated and held them. As they travelled by train to Victoria the countryside looked attractive. Eagerly they looked forward to being part of a Britain their white minister in Georgetown had described to them.

He had made little mention of what an industrial society is really like, nor had they heard of racial hostility in certain parts of England, so they were in for severe shocks. Their first surprise came at Victoria Station itself. It was so cold! Sybil's eyes focused on a white woman sweeping the platform. Until that moment she had not fully realized that they had come to an almost white society, and so received her first culture shock as she saw that white people as well as black performed menial jobs.

Before leaving Guyana they had contacted a cousin in London who had said they could stay in his flat while he was away. "I remember saying to him," Sybil recalls, "'Where is the bath?' The landlady, who was standing by us, said, 'You go out of the door, down the corridor, turn right and at the end you'll find it.' I said, 'I'm asking for the bathroom.' My cousin said, 'She's sending you to the bathroom.'"

This was Sybil's first introduction to Britain's housing problems. "The blacks in London were not like the blacks we had left back in Guyana", Sybil remembers. "In London it was a question of survival. I was not accustomed to sharing a cooker on the landing, and having no bathroom of my own, and Joe and I found the situation into which we entered was to be sheer hell."

The second shock Sybil had was in Shepherd's Bush, where they were then living. There were no crowds of people going into church! Moreover, the sight of the local clergy coming out of the pub with lighted cigarettes and in cassocks indicated a very different brand of Christianity from the Methodism Sybil had known at home.

Sybil and Joe could only stay at her cousin's for a short while, so they decided to look for alternative accommodation. Sometimes Sybil walked the streets and cried because she could not find anywhere decent to live. Once Joe and Sybil were reduced to living in a coal cellar in Lillie Road, Fulham.

It was as they searched for a home that they began to realize the racism of London. One notice read: "Room to let – lady out at business. Double-room: no dog, no children, no Irish, no coloureds need apply." It was to be the hardest part of life in England – finding a home that was decent and comfortable.

Joe and Sybil moved around much in those early months, yet despite that decided they would like to stay in Britain. The minister of their local church approached a member who had spare rooms on their behalf. One Sunday she came up to them and said: "Sybil, I feel sorry I cannot let you have a room. You see, no one in my street takes in any coloured people and I feel I cannot be the first."

Sybil was hurt, but pretended it was an incident which had not happened. Nor were they the worst off by far. Joe knew one man who was so het up about the need for accommodation he used to sleep in the parks and cinemas to save money for a house. All summer he would live very rough, and stayed at his work at Lyons till late. Here he could have a shower and wash. Really he lived nowhere, like the many who moved from place to place with their two suitcases and four boxes. When eventually he did buy his own home he put up a sign which read "No whites need apply".

Getting a job was not so difficult as finding a home in the London of the 1950s. Sybil had a number of jobs, some of them only for a short while, like working for the Citizen's Advice Bureau. She was the first black cook at Forte's "Grill and Griddle", and also did cooking for the BEA Terminal, then at West Cromwell Road. She also took in machining.

Joe was lucky indeed: he got a job with Jo Lyons and worked for them for nearly eighteen years.

The backcloth to their daily living was the Church. Methodists have a system of transfers, so it was natural for Sybil and Joe to join Shepherd's Bush Road Methodist Church when the minister there contacted Sybil, having been told of her arrival in Britain from Guyana. She became involved in the church and the community straight away, running an all-white youth club there, drawing on her experience in the club in Georgetown. It was a troubled period and Sybil felt some of the bitterness of this time.

The Notting Hill riot had occurred in 1957, and in London and elsewhere blacks and whites were beginning to feel uneasy with one another. Once a dustbin lid came through their window as one local group grew agitated and there was street fighting.

All the threads of Sybil's tapestry of life are there in these early encounters with Britain in the 1950s – her deep faith, her capacity to be enraged by white racism, her loyalty to the Church and its resources, and her understanding of and commitment to community work. If her theology was then only in its early stages her faith already had a rich strain of mysticism in it which helped her through many dark and tempestuous moments.

While they were living in Shepherd's Bush Joe and Sybil were married. Sybil was unhappy with the living accommodation and felt they needed to settle down. In preparation for the wedding she made her own suit, and one Saturday morning, with a few friends from work, she and Joe went to church and were married. Sybil then went straight home to cook the lunch, which she had put on to heat up before they left for the church service.

Sybil was not involved in politics then, her life revolving round the church and the local community. But as she worked in London she realized how exploited people in Guyana had been. She looked back to the time when she had advised white women there on codes of behaviour (do not visit a rum shop, avoid certain areas) and realized what an Upstairs/Downstairs world the 1930s in Guyana were.

Even at that time Sybil had a strong prayer life which kept her going. Indeed, she can trace this back to her childhood. There was a saying in her family that they did not want her to speak because what she said happened. "'Sybil's mouth sees further than her eyes,' said my grandfather", Sybil remembers.

The faith Sybil had received through her family, and which she claimed in that encounter with her grandfather, only grew in later years in any systematic way as she studied theology. At that time she tended to see prayer as a request for needs to be met, whereas now she would see it as communion with God as the main emphasis.

The biggest trial Sybil had at that time, which took all of her resources of prayer, was when her first baby died, and then the second, Trevor, had immediate problems with his blood, necessitating a total blood transfusion.

There was also the problem of Joe and Sybil's need of a permanent home. By 1961, when Trevor was born, they were actively seeking a solution to this problem. An English family with whom they were very friendly allowed them to stay with them for two months, while they set about buying a house which they had found in Brockley, in the borough of Deptford, as it was then called.

This couple made Sybil feel most welcome; in fact, they became god-parents to their children and were some of the many friendships Joe and Sybil made, and which enabled them to feel that their family really was in England.

Once settled in Deptford, Sybil found a task: fostering for the London Borough of Lewisham, created in the mid-1960s when the Greater London Council of thirty-two boroughs was formed. She took in first one child, then another and then a third, and her life became full with children. It meant that her own children – two more had been born, one in 1964, another in 1965 – had to share a much larger household where there was much love, but also much coming and going, as the foster children came and went over the years.

Through her growing numbers of contacts Sybil began to encourage other black women to consider fostering as well. As a mother, or aunt, or guardian (people saw her in different roles), she held nothing to be impossible – faith could and would move mountains. It was, Sybil considered, not living as such that mattered but the courage with which you lived that counted. She felt, in particular, that if young people could acquire the security of home, and had a chance to belong, then their life might take on a new meaning.

But some of those Sybil fostered needed all the forgiving resources she could muster. "I can remember," she has recalled, "once trying to separate two girls who were fighting in their bedroom. For a moment I was sure my time on earth was at an end, as one of the girls struck me with a chair leg which she had been using as her weapon in the fight. As I recovered from the blow to my head, a voice spoke

60

within my soul: 'Lo, I am with you always, even to the end.' As I came round, that inward voice steadied me and gave me renewed strength."[3]

In the 1960s Sybil was asked by her minister if she would run a youth club for the church. For the next five years she did this, as well as her fostering, giving up her night-time job in a canteen to be free to take on this new responsibility.

Then in 1967 Sybil was asked to sort out a problem at another church youth club. It ran twice a week and several hundred black young people turned up. Sybil agreed to become the leader, provided the club could have larger premises and more equipment. This led her to resign from the Methodist Club and to work every night (though paid for only two nights) for the Telegraph Hill Youth Club. Originally this had been an all-white club which a few blacks also attended and vice versa, on different nights. It was this black side which Sybil was asked to develop by the Rural Dean, Allan Auckland. He it was who held a competition to find a name for this new piece of work which Sybil had undertaken in Deptford. It was then that for the first time human beings had landed on the Moon, and the prize-winning name for the club was considered to be "Moonshot".

The Moonshot Club grew, on occasion gathering together five hundred young people in an evening. Eventually it found a home in an old run-down mission hall in Pagnell Street, in the Deptford part of Lewisham. Often tensions were high, especially between young blacks and the police and Sybil had to handle these, as well as the fights which broke out between club members.

Once a full can of Coca-Cola, thrown in a scuffle Sybil was trying to end, hit her shoulder and knocked her out. When Sybil regained consciousness she was told what had happened and that an ambulance had been called. Afraid that the police would become involved, and that the club might even be closed down, Sybil told the club members to stand her up and lean her against the wall. When the ambulance men arrived, Sybil told them to go away saying, "I'm quite all right. I don't need any help". When the men had gone, Sybil slumped to the ground again, but Moonshot was safe for the while. Sybil, however, has a shoulder pain to this day, doubtless started that night when the Coke tin hit her.

Sybil's struggles in life seem endless – one thing leads to another, and because she is always involved in a number of schemes and projects at any given moment of time, problems and difficulties seem to run concurrently. If the incident in the Moonshot Club was dealt with by forgiveness, its after-effects in Sybil's life have been dramatic. Her capacity to forgive was tested even more when it became clear, after a burglary in her home, just who had actually taken all the things which mattered most to her. "It had to be a thief just passing through the area, not knowing who lived here", she consoled herself. But it was not so. At the time she had six teenage foster girls living as part of her family, some with boyfriends. One afternoon the Community Liaison Officer for Lewisham phoned to tell Sybil that shortly she was to be visited by a detective.

The officer arrived soon after the phone call. "A boyfriend of one of my foster-girls had confessed and wanted to see me. At the Police Station I was told by the officer that nothing but the missionary box was recovered and that the family pictures had been destroyed. Before I could collect my thoughts they ushered that young man into the room; I had no difficulty recognizing him. He was a visitor to my home. For some time we just stood there, in the middle of the charge-room, looking at each other. I do not know what went through his mind, but I felt awful. All the thoughts and emotions I had suppressed for so long ebbed back to the surface. Suddenly my thieving young visitor addressed me as aunty and asked me to forgive him. I was shocked by his request. "What cheek," I thought, "forgive you!" I stormed out of the room without answering him; I needed time to cool off and to collect my thoughts. He had hurt me so badly; as a visitor to my home he had misused my trust so much, and now, after all that, without even having repaired the damage he had done, he asked me to forgive him."[4]

Sybil went home and sat down with the Bible. Did she have to forgive someone who had wronged her that much? She wanted justice! Yet the Bible was clear: she had to go and accept the apology from "my thieving young visitor" and pardon him wholeheartedly. "How small was his wrong-doing by comparison to the catalogue of guilt that I have accumulated in the eyes of God. How small by comparison is the wrong that I am asked to forgive."[5] "Forgiveness", Sybil has said, "is not holding grudges against the person responsible for a particular action. It is acceptance of what happens", and this is what she did in this, as in many other instances, in her struggle with herself to "make my own way straight as much as possible with the other person".[6]

Parallel with the fostering Sybil continued to develop Moonshot. She found herself more and more involved in community development work. The Disco she established led to her showing films from Caribbean embassies about the life of a particular country. Discussion sessions were held for members, too, based on the editorials members read in *The Times* or *The Guardian*, for young blacks needed to encounter good thinking about the society of which they were a part. In addition, homework space was offered for those who lived with a family in one room.

The Youth Service helped provide facilities when a second local child died playing in the streets. For older children Sybil started to help by assisting them to get place names correct – moving on to taking some to Parliament to see how it worked. In August, when many clubs closed, Moonshot started a holiday project for young people.

Parallel to Moonshot a mother's project was started at Pagnell Street, another piece of pioneer work, for it was the first in the country for West Indian families. It stemmed from the fact that Sybil was continually called to bail out girls who were shoplifting, or leaving their babies in their flats unattended. In the Day Centre there were cookery classes and lessons on how to cope with young children, and how to live off social security allowances and not overspend. In all this work Lewisham's medical officer for health supported Sybil.

Moonshot itself went from strength to strength. In 1973 Princess Margaret visited it, so well known had it become. "The centre was meant to serve not only blacks, but the community around it, irrespective of their colour or background", Sybil recalls. "It was to be a resource for the locality. So we also started a tenants' association."[7]

Sybil had her work cut out acting as a community and social worker and maintaining liaison with the schools, so much so that there were complaints she was only a part-time youth worker. The work it seemed had developed a dynamic of its own.

A library of "black" books was started: books by blacks, or about them. Child-minding arrangements were set up so that parents could have an occasional night off. There was also entertainment for Senior Citizens.

The football, cricket and netball teams were winning trophies, but improved facilities were needed. This was so not only for them, but also for the classes in mechanics, woodwork, photography, the arts and academic subjects. An extension was planned, and in 1977 an appeal launched, the same year that the Prince of Wales visited the club. By the middle of November an article had appeared in a national newspaper saying that the National Front had held a meeting and was determined to burn down the building.

"On 18th December," Sybil has recalled, "I was called out out at four in the morning by the police. I shall never forget the blaze of red flames. It was the time of the firemen's strike and the inadequacy of the military "green goddesses" and their soldier crews was only too evident. The young soldiers handling the hoses had my complete sympathy."[8] Acting on impulse Sybil rushed forward and struggled past the broken door to get inside. "The firemen were furious, but she had to see if there was anything left to salvage. In particular she wanted to get 'the books'. These were the accounts for the Centre and they showed how much money had been collected and spent. If they were lost it would mean hours and hours of extra work. She found the books, soaking wet, charred but safe, in a cupboard half melted by the heat of the fire."[9]

It was a severe test of Sybil's faith, yet she vowed, "My name is Phoenix, and, so help me God, out of the ashes I will rebuild Moonshot." She did, and in March 1981 it was opened by His Royal Highness, the Prince of Wales.

"What comes out clearly from such experiences", Sybil has written, "is that our trust in God must not be unrealistic. As Mother Julian reminds us, God never promises that we shall not be tempted; but he does promise us the strength not to be overcome by the temptation. I have grown to realize that my work is not mine; rather I am to work in God's service and in fellowship with him."[10]

While Sybil and Joe were involved in public work in the 1960s and 1970s, culminating in the re-opening of Moonshot, their private life knew a deep sadness. The year 1973 was one which stretched all members of the family to the limit, both in its capacity to forgive God for the hurts we experience and in its capacity to live with the fallibility we all possess. During that summer Sybil took a group of young people, including her own children, on holiday in Kent. One afternoon, driving back from the beach, with most of the young people in the coach, and a few with Sybil in the car, a motorcyclist came towards her on the wrong side of the road. Sybil swerved to avoid the rider and her car left the road and hit a telegraph pole. Sybil's daughter, Marsha, was killed in the crash. Sybil herself was badly hurt, leaving her with a difficulty in walking to this day as a result of the injuries she received then.

Never before had Joe and Sybil needed such support. But a good thing came from this tragedy. "During the years she had been working in Lewisham . . . Sybil had become aware that many white people disliked black people. White people, she felt, treated black people badly; they would not give them jobs, talk to them politely or accept them as equal members of the community."[11] It had made Sybil bitter. Now among those who gave Sybil and Joe support were members of many churches who knew of Sybil's work. Sybil felt her bitterness melting away.

Her community needed Sybil, so though she felt angry and confused and found forgiveness difficult, she was pulled back to work in the community because of its deep needs. And six years later, in November 1979, a home was opened for the Phoenix foster-children in memory of her daughter. The two houses, made into one, stood immediately opposite Sybil and Joe's house in Tressillian Road, SE4. "Faith", Sybil has argued, "gives you hope, which allows you to change the negative influences to positive energies. For example, anger, which can be so negative, can become the drive to change things."[12] There before her in the new home, supported with funds from Lewisham Borough Council and elsewhere, was the living proof of Sybil and Joe's capacity to bring something redemptive out of suffering, even though the cost of forgiveness for both of them was high in this situation.

On 18th January 1981, at a house in Deptford where a party was taking place, thirteen young black people were burned to death. Tension in Deptford rose again, was this another act of racists?, people asked. Many, not only in London but across the United Kingdom, thought it was. Mystery still hangs over the fire and the open verdict that the courts declared about its start, but there is no mystery about Sybil's role in ministering to the people whose lives were so drastically altered by it. Nor is Sybil quiet about her struggle to forgive those she felt had been less than honest and courageous in getting to the root causes of that fire.

Immediately, Sybil took in some of the people intimately affected, as well as their relatives, and set about comforting the bereaved, identifying five of the bodies for their grieving relatives. Funerals had to be arranged, and Sybil and her friends found money to pay the funeral bills for some. Talking to Sybil today she still hurts. "Oh that fire, that fire! It is still burning within me", she exclaims. "I am hurting for the non-responsibility for the ones that were left by society at large", she explains. "For I cannot remain indifferent. I am living with the hurt and the anger of that, and the families in and out of mental hospitals. Had we not been the untouchables of society we would have been treated differently. Look how those involved in the Zeebrugge, King's Cross and Hungerford disasters have been helped."

It is hardly surprising that Sybil feels this way, for it was she who organized the Memorial Service in Westminster Central Hall on 17th May 1981 for the thirteen young people who died in the New Cross Fire. And it has been Sybil Phoenix who since then has kept in touch with the families who have suffered so much from that moment up to now. And it has been Sybil, too, who has regularly attended the Annual Memorial Services, preaching at two of them. "At the end of the day," a friend of Sybil's has said, "when all the tos and fros of the Deptford Fire have been argued, what people saw was Sybil supporting the black families. Probably it is only Sybil who is still involved. If the campaigners were over-critical of her it says more about *them* than about Sybil."[13]

After the Deptford Fire Sybil and the families

whose children died received hate mail. Indeed, over the years she and her family have suffered many attacks which have stretched their capacity for forgiveness to the limit. More than once Sybil has gone to her car to find paint has been poured over it, or the tyres slashed. There have been threatening phone calls, too, in the middle of the night, and at one time the police, fearing she might be attacked, put a guard on her house and arranged for phone calls to be intercepted.

Though angry and at times afraid, Sybil does not seem to end up hating those who attack her. "You cannot hate and love", she has said. And Sybil wants so much to love, so she finds she has to wrestle with the meaning of forgiveness. "Forgiveness", she considers, "is about loving not hating." This does not mean, however, that Sybil does not get angry, for she does. And on occasions her temper gets the better of her. Then she has to wrestle with herself and with God, as she has done over the times when she and her family have been seriously threatened. "Forgiveness in Christ – that's where I find my being", she reflects. "When I am trying to give as good as I get, because I am trying to be a follower of His, I think, 'That's not how he would have handled it.'"

The result of this wrestling with God has been to make Sybil grow in love and concern to such an extent that in most of the London Borough of Lewisham she is highly regarded: indeed she has become one of its most illustrious citizens.

"I was talking to some workers," Sybil has reflected, "saying one needs a lot of forgiving to be able to cope with the community. You have to become a 'big' person, in the sense of beyond yourself, in that it doesn't matter what people say any more. You are in this community to serve it, regardless of how you are treated . . . You remember the ambiguities of people, how one minute they need you, the next you are forgotten or abused, but you cannot afford to keep the memory alive of what has been said. I remember", she recalls, "the things people wrote when I accepted the MBE which were poisonous. But the MBE has served the community far more than me personally and now this is recognized. The wheel has come full circle now." You have to keep your lines of communication to people open, she feels, and not block them up with hate.

"I can remember," she says of a particularly painful experience at the heart of her life, "trying not to hate someone who had caused me grief. I spent two days asking not to hate this person." Immense damage had been done in a piece of work in which they had both been engaged. Eventually the person left. Later she returned, asking for her job back. "Like a fool," says Sybil, "I gave it back. I felt you cannot personalize your life in society. I know this person could do the job, so made the appointment. I could not see why I couldn't forgive the wrong that had been done."

This did not prevent a further hurt, however. Yet when there was trouble in that woman's family Sybil was rung up and asked for prayers. Her colleague was at Sybil's commissioning service as a Methodist lay preacher, apologizing for what had been done in the past.

By the time Moonshot was opened again Sybil's work had developed in another direction as she toured Britain talking and preaching in a strenuous ministry. Her local community work gave her talks, sermons and lectures an authenticity and a grass-roots feel. "The David Frost Show" (1973), "Thought for

70

the Day" (1974), TV debate with Joan Lestor on the future of education in Britain, also in the early 1970s, where Sybil argued for the need to re-write some history books, were among the many media events in which she had taken part in the previous decade. Pagnell Street in its early days, too, had drawn much media attention and given Sybil a high profile. Now she was in great demand as an interpreter to many sections of society of how blacks felt, especially in the inner cities. Whether it has been addressing the Women's section of the Labour Party at Brighton one year in the 1970s, or being one of a panel who knew Prince Charles and were invited the night before his marriage to talk about him (and his work in the community), Sybil has seized the opportunities as they have come, to speak on behalf of blacks in Britain. Each occasion has a different flavour – thus what she says on "Home on Sunday" is distinct from her contribution to the TV Panel on "The Limits of Forgiveness" (chaired by Bruce Kent), but in essence her task is always the same: to interpret to society how blacks feel.

With her long track record of involvement in community relations, starting with the Southwark Diocesan Race Relations Group, when she speaks people feel that what she says comes out of a long-standing concern and experience. This work, especially in its relation to forgiveness, can best be understood in her work with the police. For four or five years she organized an annual party for elderly West Indians, with police cadets helping with the meals. For two years at Moonshot there was a Christmas Party, when members of Lewisham Police were invited to play Father Christmas. Sybil also organized an annual party with a focus on deaf and dumb people to which others would come, including police officers.

The police of Lewisham also come to Marsha Phoenix house for a six-week course in community relations. When police officers talk to the girls they often invite them to visit the dog training school. It is all an attempt by Sybil to build bridges, often when there is considerable fear. "Because we live here we have to work with the police", she argues, when people challenge this aspect of her work. She considers that people need to see the police as friends in case of trouble. Moreover, being a police officer for Sybil means ". . . washing the blood off the road, finding a dead body . . ." and the community must support this work.

It can be fairly said that Sybil has been a forerunner in organizing police/community liaison groups, for even as far back as the 1960s she was at work building bridges. In the early 1970s she was involved in discussions with police at the Scotland Yard level, about the setting up of Help on Arrest schemes. This involved finding people in the community who could be called on to be with those held but not charged, so that such people could know their rights before making a statement to the police. This was eventually taken into the work of community relations, which led to Police/Community Liaison Officers being appointed.

From 1968 onwards Sybil regularly visited the Hendon Police Training School for training sessions with police cadets, a commitment involving six weekly sessions. While this scheme lasted, Sybil would lecture on how to deal with communities other than their own, or how newcomers to British society felt. She used to consider issues of stability and change, looking at how society was able to handle and sustain the changes which were occurring. Could Britain respond positively to these changes, she would ask. What stresses were being put on the newcomers, and with what result? She repeated the lectures at the South London Cadet Training School.

Even though Lewisham has had bad police officers – which Sybil readily admits – she will also maintain it has good officers, too. "I have found I have to remain friends with the police," she says, "if I was to serve the community."

When Sybil was Vice-Chairman of the Lewisham Council for Community Relations, for two or three years, she was the person who was regularly called when problems arose during the evening. Later two or three others were also put on the "On Call" list. This was one of the first schemes to involve community leaders in such consultative work.

"I have no choice but to work with the police", Sybil repeats, but knowing that human nature is not perfect and that there will always be disagreements over specific incidents. Sometimes "we have agreed to disagree but remain friends", she observes. This has applied to a number of issues over the years, where police and the black community have clashed, and there have been rival interpretations of what has happened.

This has been especially true where allegations of racism in the police have been made, an issue of which Sybil is most aware, and which increasingly has claimed her attention. Over a decade of preaching, speaking and lecturing, and involvement with students from Oxford, Cambridge and elsewhere (all of whom have come to work with her in south

London), Sybil has become more and more aware of the need for training in racism perspectives.

"Racism permeates every part of British society," says the Introduction to *With You in Spirit?*, the Report a group of which Sybil was a member, made to Cardinal Hume, advising him on the Catholic Church's commitment to the black community.

"There is no area of society in Britain where it is not experienced by black people", the report maintained. "Peace is the fruit of justice. There will be no peace until a proper balance of racial justice is achieved." It is this central awareness which has led Sybil increasingly into programmes to train people to become more aware of racism in the structures of British society.

In 1981, therefore, she left the newly opened Pagnell Street Centre and started to work at Clubland, the Methodist Church in Camberwell, where she became director of MELRAW (Methodist Leadership Racism Awareness Workshop). This involved her in running weekend conferences and courses to help people understand the human family and its essential unity, regardless of background, or colour. It took Sybil to many places, including suburban areas, to lead courses on black/white relations.

Sybil saw this work in a community context. "I'm a community worker," she maintains, "that's my politics. I started training because I felt people needed to be aware of the kind of hurts they inflict on black people. I've come to handling it differently because I am now aware it's the English education and upbringing which has made them as they are. Home, peer group, makes them racist. I've come to realize this as I worked with people over the years."

74

"The training I now do is different from the beginning. I'm working out of people's experience. I personally believe if you're not racist as a white person your education failed you. You've had to work at being anti-racist, for you are brought up to feel better than those who live down the road."[14]

Though it all began in embryo in the 1960s when Sybil organized workshops for social workers, teachers and ministers, because she felt they needed to know about the problems of black children, it was only now in the 1980s that her teaching, through MELRAW, had a bite to the training. "I am not asking anybody for equality," Sybil has asserted, "because I am born equal. There isn't anyone, anywhere, who isn't", she adds defiantly.[15]

Sybil feels that now white society has begun to listen to what happens to black people in a white environment Christians especially need to work at their vocation: loving their neighbour as themselves. "Until they can love their neighbour, their black brothers and sisters whom Christ also died for, until they take that commandment seriously, they're not full Christians."

What then becomes of equal opportunity policies of governments and local authorities, or racism awareness training programmes themselves? "Black people in churches, in society, are denied their humanity by being told that they have to have an equal opportunities policy; no church has any right to have Race Relations – but because we have lost our way, we've got to become aware of the sin of racism and ask for forgiveness. We as black people who take up the Cross have a lot of work to do in educating society."[16]

Here Sybil seems to move from personal forgiveness to a more corporate sense of righting wrongs.

75

Though the two cannot be totally divorced there is surely a different dimension to corporate wrongdoing. Perhaps what Sybil is really doing is to help other people to come to terms with things in their own lives. The public figure that people see in lectures and courses and on the media is forged out of private experience, often of a most painful kind. Perhaps what Sybil does here in public is to mediate forgiveness both ways, from the black community to the white, and vice versa, by the authentic way she speaks of the matter, and of her own struggles to be forgiving.

"Our work", noted Vic Watson, Chairman of Sybil's group, "is about strengthening Christian conviction that racism is theologically heretical, morally indefensible, legally wrong and politically contemptible."[17] To that work Sybil Phoenix brought not only her flair and twenty years or more as a community worker, but a mind stored with material from the diverse reading in which she engages. On her shelves are to be found John Taylor's *The Go-Between God*, or the black American John Perkins' *Let Justice Roll Down*. Also on the shelves is Albert Luthuli's *Let My People Go*. (Each Christmas Sybil has held a carol concert to raise money for deprived communities in South Africa.) Other reading material includes Jürgen Moltmann's *The Church in the Power of the Spirit* and Dietrich Bonhoeffer's *Ethics*. ("Bonhoeffer is one of my favourite persons", says Sybil.) It is not surprising to find her reading James Cone's *God of the Oppressed*, nor to find that she reads much black theology and books on the role of women in the church and in society.

Behind all this reading and working is Sybil, the woman of prayer. She is a public person in political life in the widest sense of the word (a lunch at 10,

Downing Street, making meals for guests at her south-east London home, or raising money to send people to Guyana to find their roots are all taken in her stride). But the focus for all this is her life hidden with Christ in God. "Sybil has a tremendous capacity for loving in the face of hatred, rejection and discrimination", says Vic Watson. It is clear that it is the forgiving, overpowering love of God in her which makes this possible.

In his review of a short biography of Sybil prepared for schoolchildren Paul Lazenby has commented: "The admissions of bitterness towards white people (for their racism), towards God (for the loss of a daughter) and fear of racial attacks present Sybil Phoenix not as someone whose life should be put on a pedestal and admired as some kind of unattainable ideal, but rather as an inspiration to others to show similar love and devotion to God despite their own human weaknesses."[18]

As David Sheppard, Bishop of Liverpool, has also written: "I have spent evenings in the Moonshot Club, other times in her home and twenty-four hours with a group of young people who told her they wanted to meet some church leaders. I felt something of the frustration and anger of young black people at the exclusion from opportunities which they experience. Sybil Phoenix soaks up these bitter feelings every day. Soaking it up means that it stops with her; she doesn't pass it on by adding to the chain of reaction of bitterness." She does this by centring her life in prayer and trust in Christ. "He lets her share in his pain," the Bishop continues, "when he soaked up the sin and hatred of people he loved."[19]

"There can be no reconciliation without forgiveness", Sybil has written. "We must recognize our sin – disobedience to God; then receive forgiveness through the sacrifice of Christ. We need to ponder two things in this area – one is the absolute and complete nature of God's forgiveness. The second is the *cost* of God's forgiveness."[20]

It is this root to Sybil's work which makes her a puzzle to people in secular politics, who are not used to religion as an overt factor in community work. What makes it possible for a black woman to be accepted in a white world? She seems to have "made it", blacks comment, and yet others are left behind.

This surely is a wrong way to understand Sybil Phoenix. Essentially she is a natural mystic, drawn by the cord of God's love into public life, there to work and witness. The root of all her work lies in her Christian discipleship. Its fruits are a welter of community action and personal caring too great in scope to be enumerated in detail here. It is this authenticity of life which gives Sybil access to people in the structures, both regional and national.

She is a do-er, and people know that for all her organizational faults her life has been both tried and tested, even in the most intimate family areas. "You cannot go through life not forgiving, some time, some place", her husband Joe has said. It could well be Sybil's motto, too, for as Joe maintains, and his wife has demonstrated, "You can't live without forgiveness".

"Sometimes," Sybil has written, "I wish I could become invisible, so that those who reject me because of my colour would be directly confronted with God's love . . . only by establishing God's love in the hearts of human beings can we change the course of history."[21]

78

That is the testimony of a disciple who above all has been seized and grasped by a love mightier than her own. How can one paint a picture of this unusual woman, who has grown to such stature since those first early days in West London described at the start of this narrative? Perhaps the best way is to let the words of a young black woman who has known her only since 1979 be the final eloquent testimony to Sybil's character, grace and effectiveness.

"I was impressed by a number of things", she has said. "By the respect she received from white people and by the background papers for Moonshot, and by her links with County Hall. She has an enormous ability to encourage and help others to do things. She is humble and will not think of mentioning her involvement in getting a course going at Goldsmith's College. Her background and belief enable her to do all sorts of things regardless of the pain she feels when black people comment on her getting on, or who feel her approach is not right. She should not be loving and forgiving. In Britain you should stand and fight.

"Sybil is a giver, she gives herself totally, but why when she has so much suffering both in public and in private life? It is simply that she loves people.

"Yet she is street-wise – she understands young people's lives and views. At a party she can even enable a wide variety of people to respond to a prayer, or even a hymn!"

"Even when she makes mistakes or cannot live up to people's expectations of her people say, 'You cannot fault her on the main issues – caring for blacks, and taking up issues'."

"She is, moreover, good at giving others access to the power she has. She is highly intelligent and intuitively sharp but can ask advice when needing to do writing. It is fascinating to know how many forms she's helped fill in!"

"Her political analysis is not only about consciousness-raising. She makes sure there are real practical outcomes to her work. A number of Councillors, for example, relate to her both personally and publicly. She is not a masculine woman – you know she cries for real in a situation.

"Sybil has made many blacks and whites open their eyes to realities of which they were not aware. She never loses sight of the fact that she is a black woman – that's the political edge. Her life is about identification as a black woman. She has a clear analysis of what it is to be black in this society. The most unlikely people have been touched by Sybil: they will not forget her. Having been able to touch her life I've gone away and changed in many ways.

"Once a mini-cab had been ordered," her friend concludes, "for Sybil to go to see Prince Charles, who had asked to meet her. Sybil had not good clothes on, for she had been cleaning. A friend offered to let her change into her clothes. Sybil let the friend go upstairs to change, then quietly slipped away in the taxi unchanged, and undismayed."[22]

Sybil is a deeply caring person who is surprising "and also a toughie", she sums up. A measure of the depth of that caring can be seen finally in two incidents from the 1970s. One relates to a couple who threw a bottle which landed on Sybil's head. Sybil took the

80

glass out and kept the person who threw the bottle at her house, then paid for the cab to take her to her friend. "I couldn't do any different. Every time I have to turn a girl out I suffer. I ask, have I done enough for her? What kind of trouble have I turned her out into?"

The second incident involves Joe too. After the Moonshot fire they both toured the pubs and other meeting places of the area, to try to calm the angry black young people who had nowhere to meet until an alternative site was found while the re-building programme got underway. Had they not assuaged the flames of hate by their forgiveness who knows where the resentment might have led?

"The heat will never be off the black community", Sybil explains with her customary realism. The police and the blacks have the same problem, she thinks, both being minority groups, and easily identifiable. Easily, too, they can become the target of the criticism of others.

Yet Sybil is determined not to leave any situation with that degree of polarization. Prince Charles once said of Sybil that she was a "shuttlecock". She does – not only with the police and the black community, but with other groups – mediate forgiveness both ways and can therefore be battered by both sides. But she is determined to go on praying, struggling, forgiving, working for change.

"If we are centred on ourselves," she argues, "the smallest risk is too great for us because both success and failure can destroy us. If we are centred upon God, no risk is too great, because success is already guaranteed."[23]

Notes: Sybil Phoenix

1. *Willing Hands*, Sybil Phoenix (The Bible Reading Fellowship 1984) p. 13
2. *Living in Harmony*, John Newbury (Religious and Moral Education Press 1985) p. 6
3. *Willing Hands*, Sybil Phoenix (The Bible Reading Fellowship 1984) p. 23
4. Ibid p. 33
5. Ibid p. 35
6. Interview with Sybil Phoenix
7. *Willing Hands*, Sybil Phoenix (The Bible Reading Fellowship 1984) p. 38
8. Ibid p. 40
9. *Living in Harmony*, John Newbury (Religious and Moral Education Press 1985) pp. 18–19
10. *Willing Hands*, Sybil Phoenix (Bible Reading Fellowship 1984) p. 40
11. *Living in Harmony*, John Newbury (Religious and Moral Education Press 1985) p. 16
12. *Willing Hands*, Sybil Phoenix (The Bible Reading Fellowship 1984) pp 25–6
13. Interview with Beverly Alexander, Autumn 1987
14. Sybil Phoenix, "Thorn in the Side of the Church", *Racial Justice* No 5 Winter 1986, pp. 6–7
15. Ibid
16. Ibid
17. Vic Watson in "An Introduction to Racism Awareness Training" – A Discussion Paper by Tony Holden (MELRAW, 54 Camberwell Road, SE 5 OEN)

18. Paul Lazenby in Review of *Living in Harmony* by John Newbury, *Racial Justice* No 5 Winter 1986, p. 22

19. The Rt Rev. David Sheppard in the Introduction to *Willing Hands* (Bible Reading Fellowship 1984)

20. Ibid p. 31

21. Ibid p. 46

22. Interview with Beverly Alexander, Autumn 1987

23. *Willing Hands*, Sybil Phoenix (Bible Reading Fellowship 1984) p. 46

Interviews with Sybil Phoenix, as the quote from 6 above, were held over a number of years. The quotations in the text come from two held in 1987 and 1988 and earlier interviews in the first half of the 1980s.

Fount Paperbacks

Fount is one of the leading paperback publishers of religious books and below are some of its recent titles.

- ☐ FRIENDSHIP WITH GOD David Hope £2.95
- ☐ THE DARK FACE OF REALITY Martin Israel £2.95
- ☐ LIVING WITH CONTRADICTION Esther de Waal £2.95
- ☐ FROM EAST TO WEST Brigid Marlin £3.95
- ☐ GUIDE TO THE HERE AND HEREAFTER
  Lionel Blue/Jonathan Magonet £4.50
- ☐ CHRISTIAN ENGLAND (1 Vol) David Edwards £10.95
- ☐ MASTERING SADHANA Carlos Valles £3.95
- ☐ THE GREAT GOD ROBBERY George Carey £2.95
- ☐ CALLED TO ACTION Fran Beckett £2.95
- ☐ TENSIONS Harry Williams £2.50
- ☐ CONVERSION Malcolm Muggeridge £2.95
- ☐ INVISIBLE NETWORK Frank Wright £2.95
- ☐ THE DANCE OF LOVE Stephen Verney £3.95
- ☐ THANK YOU, PADRE Joan Clifford £2.50
- ☐ LIGHT AND LIFE Grazyna Sikorska £2.95
- ☐ CELEBRATION Margaret Spufford £2.95
- ☐ GOODNIGHT LORD Georgette Butcher £2.95
- ☐ GROWING OLDER Una Kroll £2.95

All Fount Paperbacks are available at your bookshop or newsagent, or they can be ordered by post from Fount Paperbacks, Cash Sales Department, G.P.O. Box 29, Douglas, Isle of Man. Please send purchase price plus 22p per book, maximum postage £3. Customers outside the UK send purchase price, plus 22p per book. Cheque, postal order or money order. No currency.

NAME (Block letters) _____

ADDRESS_____

_____

_____